Phonics and Spelling

2

Julie Crimmins-Crocker

Published by Collins
An imprint of HarperCollins*Publishers*
77–85 Fulham Palace Road
Hammersmith
London
W6 8JB

**Browse the complete Collins catalogue at
www.collinseducation.com**

© HarperCollins*Publishers* Limited 2011, on behalf of the author
First published in 2007 by Folens Limited.

ISBN-13: 978-0-00-743699-6

Julie Crimmins-Crocker asserts her moral right to be identified as the author of this work.

Any educational institution that has purchased one copy of this publication may make unlimited duplicate copies for use exclusively within that institution. Permission does not extend to reproduction, storage within a retrieval system, or transmittal in any form or by any means, electronic, mechanical, photocopying, recording or otherwise, of duplicate copies for loaning, renting or selling to any other institution without the permission of the Publisher.

British Library Cataloguing in Publication Data
A catalogue record for this publication is available from the British Library.

Every effort has been made to trace copyright holders and to obtain their permission for the use of copyright material. The authors and publishers will gladly receive any information enabling them to rectify any error or omission in subsequent editions.

Managing editor: Joanne Mitchell
Layout artist: Neil Hawkins, ndesignuk.co.uk
Illustrations: JB Illustrations; Bob Farley of GCI; Helen Jackson, Nicola Pearce and Peter Wilks of SGA; Colin King; Tony Randell and Leonie Shearing c/o Lucas Alexander Whitley.
Cover design: Blayney Partnership

Printed and bound by Hobbs the Printers Ltd, Totton, Hampshire.

Contents

This contents list provides an overview of the learning objectives of each puzzle page.

Tips for teachers	3
What's next?	4
Know your phonemes	5
Alphabetical order	8
Words that begin with **bl**, **cl**, **fl**, **gl**, **pl** and **sl**	16
Words that begin with **cr**, **dr**, **fr**, **gr**, **pr** and **tr**	17
Words that begin with **dw**, **sw** and **tw**	18
Words that begin with **sc**, **sk**, **sm**, **sn**, **sp** and **st**	19
Words that begin with two phonemes blended together	20
Words that begin with **ch**, **sh** and **th**	22
Words that begin with **scr** and **spl**	23
Words that begin with **spr** and **squ**	24
Words that begin with **str**	25
Words that begin with **scr**, **spl**, **spr** and **str**	26
Words that begin with **thr**	27
Words that begin with **thr** and **shr**	28
Words that begin with **scr**, **spl**, **spr**, **squ**, **str** and **thr**	29
The blends **ch**, **ph** and **wh**	30
Words that rhyme	31
Words that end in **ld**, **nd** and **rd**	38
Words that end in **lk**, **nk** and **rk**	39
Words that end in **lm** and **rm**	40
Words that end in **lp**, **mp**, **rp** and **sp**	41
Words that end in **ct**, **ft**, **lt**, **nt**, **rt** and **st**	42
Words that end in **nch**, **rch** and **tch**	43
Words that end in **ff**, **ll**, **ss**, **ck** and **ng**	44
Words that end in **ck**	45
Words that end in **ng**	46
Hard and soft **g**	47
The **ai** phoneme spelt **ay**	48
The **ai** phoneme	49
Words that rhyme using the **ai** phoneme	50
The **ee** phoneme	51
Words that rhyme using the **ee** phoneme	52
The **igh** phoneme	53
Words that rhyme using the **igh** phoneme	55
The **oa** phoneme	56
Words that rhyme using the **oa** phoneme	57
The long **oo** phoneme	58
Words that rhyme using the long **oo** phoneme	59
Words with **ar**	60
Words with **aw**	61
The **ur** phoneme	62
Words with **ea**	63
Words with **air**, **are**, **ear** and **ere**	64
Words with **ow**	65
Words with **oo**	66
The **oi** phoneme	67
The **or** phoneme	68
Plurals	69
Adding **ed**	70
Adding **ing**	71
Words that end in **y**	72
Words with double letters	73
Words with **er**	74
Words with **ly**	75
Syllables	76
Compound words	77
Things at school (nouns)	78
Things in the garden (nouns)	79
Opposites (antonyms)	80
Words with **un** and **dis**	81
High frequency words	82
High frequency words in sentences	83
High frequency words – how many letters?	84
Sorting high frequency words by first phoneme	85
What can aliens do? (verbs)	86
How do aliens feel? (adjectives)	87
Upper and lower case letters	88
Upper case letters	89
Answers	90

Tips for teachers

Practise with Puzzles can be used alongside any existing phonics programme. The puzzles are an enjoyable and practical way to:

- introduce the phonemes and basic spelling concepts of the English language;
- provide valuable practice, to consolidate the children's knowledge of phonemes and spelling concepts and also to enhance their confidence;
- provide support activities for less able children;
- provide a challenge for more able children;
- provide formative data to assess the children's achievement levels and future learning needs.

Here are some ideas to make the puzzle sessions more enjoyable and successful:

- First, introduce the children to the phonemes or words covered in the puzzle.
- Demonstrate what the phonemes and words look like and sound like.
- Give the children plenty of oral practice in saying the phonemes, blending the phonemes and saying the words.
- Relate the phonemes to other words they know, for example, items in the classroom and at home that also have the same phoneme, rhyme, first phoneme, last phoneme and so on.
- Give the children practice in writing the phonemes using a range of tactile materials, for example, sand, whiteboards, crayons, paints and Plasticine.
- Practise writing the phonemes 'in the air' and with pencil and paper, ensuring correct pencil grip and sitting posture.
- Read through the title, introduction and instructions for each puzzle to ensure the children know what to do.
- Provide the children with the equipment they need for each puzzle (or ensure they know where to access this equipment), for example, pencils, coloured crayons, scissors, glue and so on.
- Provide additional support for children who need it, by filling in letters and/or more challenging words/answers prior to photocopying.
- Some puzzles also have word banks that can be omitted to make the puzzles more challenging, if appropriate.
- After completion of the puzzle, introduce the children to 'What's next?' (see page 4) which outlines valuable reinforcement and extension activities. Depending on the children's ability, they could either choose an activity or complete one as directed by the teacher. (The activities vary in difficulty and should be selected as appropriate.)
- 'What's next?' could be photocopied and stuck in children's literacy books to provide a record of the activities they have completed.

What's next?

Use the words in the puzzles you have done to complete these activities.

Activity	Puzzle title	Date
Practise your handwriting. Write each phoneme or word five times in your book.		
Practise writing the words and then draw a picture for each one.		
Find three more words that begin with the same phoneme. For example, *cap, cat, cut,* all begin with **c**.		
Find three more words that begin with the same blend of phonemes. For example, *flag, flip, flop,* all begin with **fl**.		
Find five more words that end with the same phoneme. For example, *cat, hit, but, wet, net,* all end with **t**.		
Find three more words that end with the same blend of phonemes. For example, *fast, fist, post,* all end with **st**.		
Find three more words that rhyme.		
Sort the words into alphabetical order and put them in a list.		
Put the words into sentences. Remember to start with a capital letter and end with a full stop.		
Put the words into sentences that are questions. Remember to start with a capital letter and end with a question mark. For example, *Where is my cat?*		
Find opposites (called **antonyms**) for the words and write them in pairs or groups. For example, *big – small*.		
Sort the words into groups with the same number of syllables.		

Know your phonemes

Blend the phonemes to read the words. Circle the phoneme in each word that is the same as the phoneme in the star. One has been done for you.

☆ b	(b)ed rub black	☆ h	hen hat hop
☆ c	cat cut club	☆ j	jam jog jet
☆ d	dog bed drum	☆ l	leg ball clap
☆ f	fox fat flag	☆ m	mop jam plum
☆ g	go bug green	☆ n	nut hen run

Know your phonemes

Blend the phonemes to read the words. Circle the phoneme in each word that is the same as the phoneme in the star.

★			
p	peg	cup	pit
qu	queen	quick	quack
r	rat	rain	tree
s	sun	yes	sail
t	tap	pet	trip
v	vet	vest	have
w	wet	we	went
x	box	fix	fox
y	yes	yelp	you
z	zip	zoo	zebra

Know your phonemes

Blend the phonemes to read the words in each rocket. Circle the phoneme in each word that is the same as the phoneme in the star. One has been done for you.

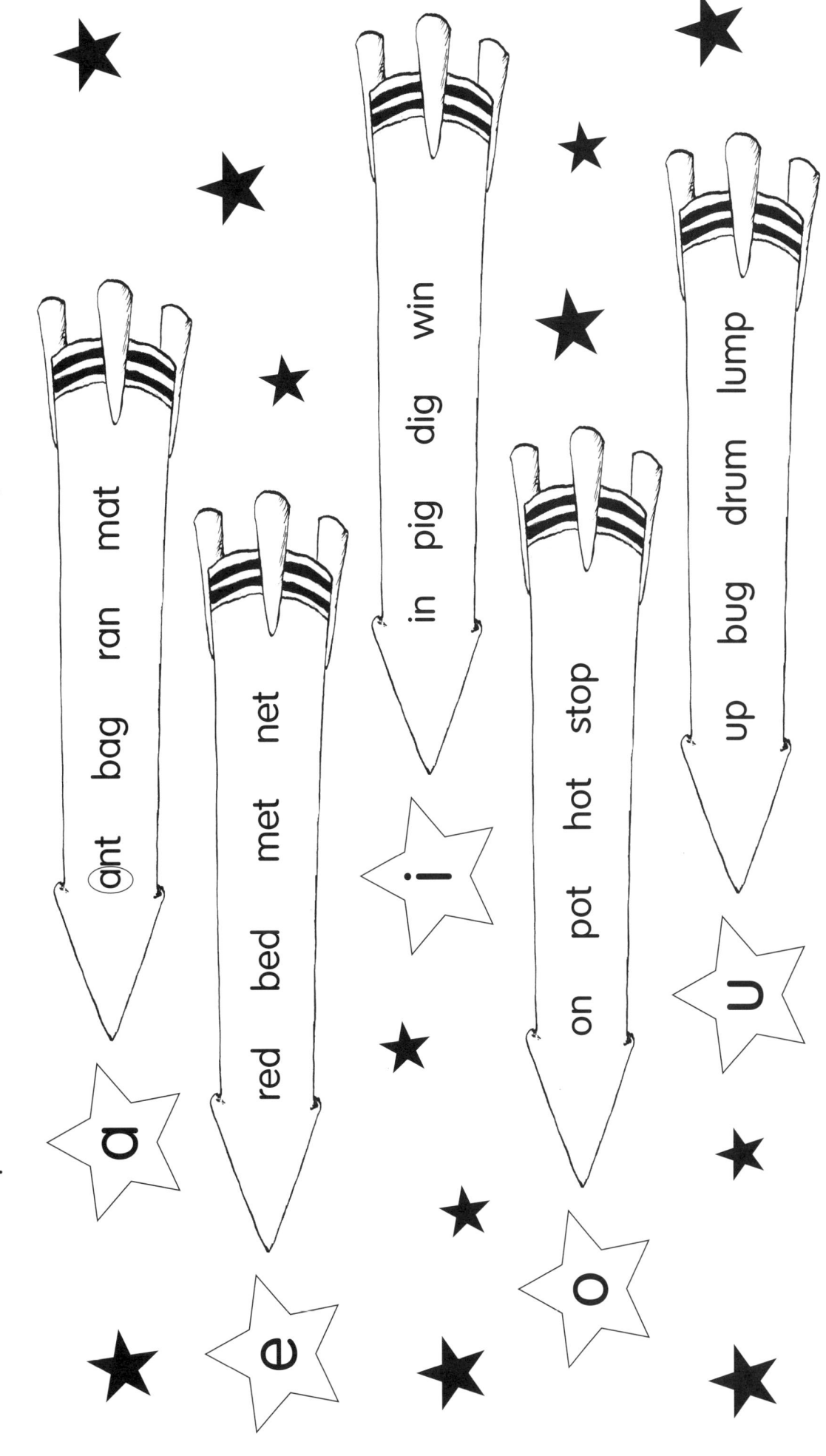

Rocket 1: (ant) bag ran mat — star: a
Rocket 2: red bed met net — star: e
Rocket 3: in pig dig win — star: i
Rocket 4: on pot hot stop — star: o
Rocket 5: up bug drum lump — star: u

Alphabetical order

Write the missing letters in the footprints so that they are in alphabetical order. The missing letters that you need are in the spaceships.

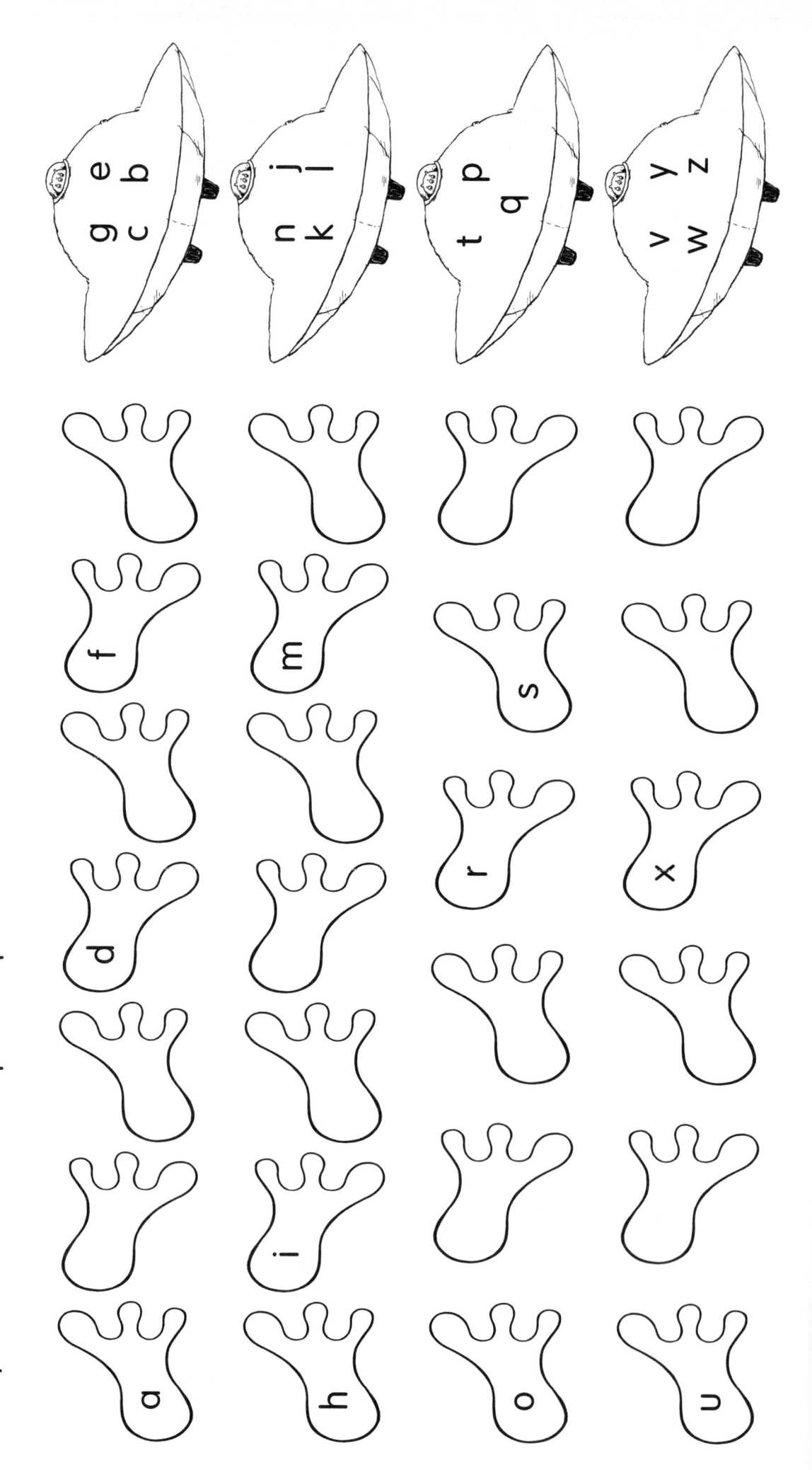

Spaceships:
- b c e g
- j k l n
- p q t
- v w y z

Footprints (in order): a, _, _, d, _, f, _, h, i, _, _, _, m, _, o, _, _, r, s, _, _, _, _, _, _, u, _, _, _, x, _, _

Alphabetical order

Put these letters into alphabetical order and write them in the stars.

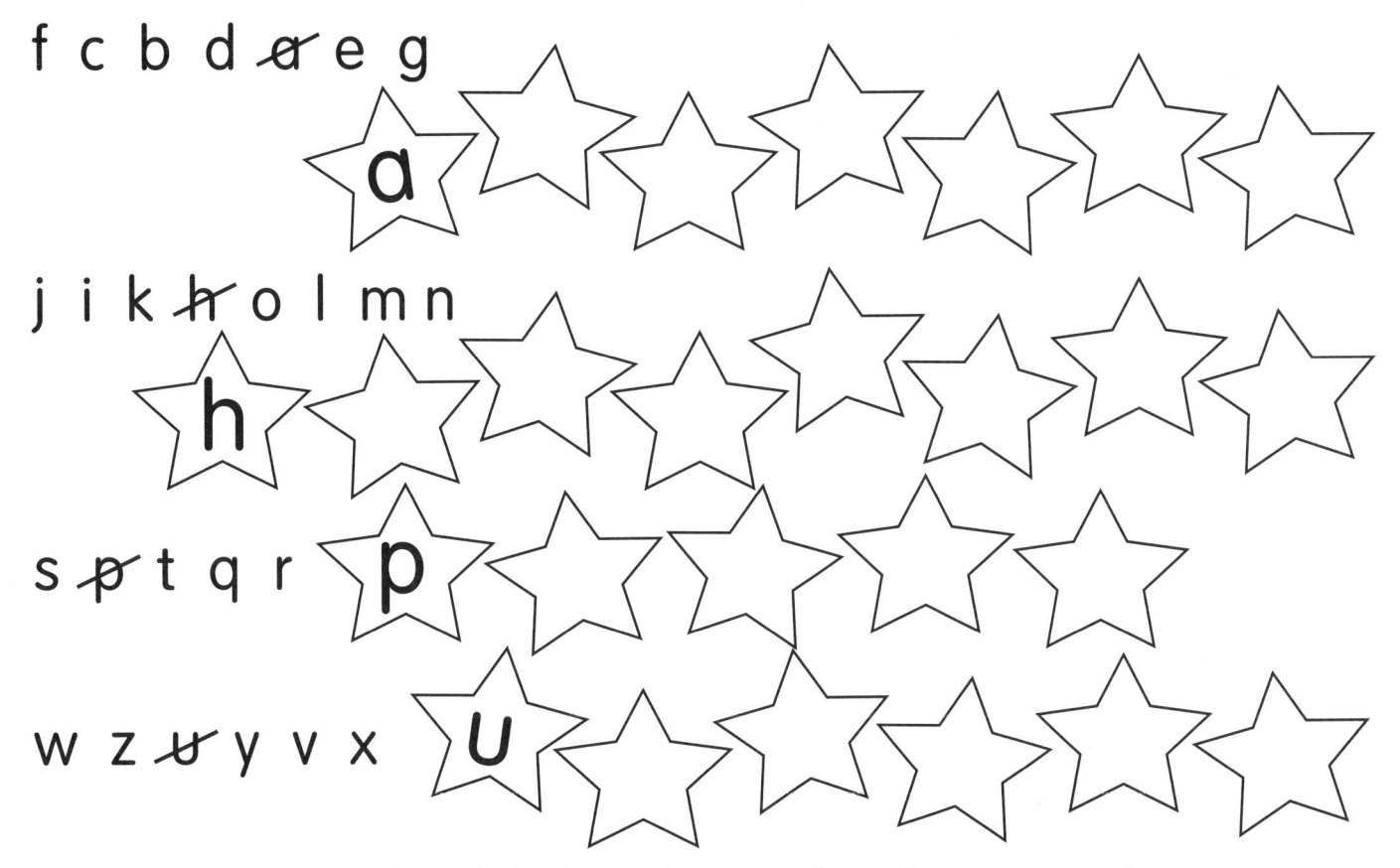

f c b d ~~a~~ e g

a

j i k ~~h~~ o l m n

h

s ~~p~~ t q r p

w z ~~u~~ y v x u

Fill in the gaps in the alphabet alien snake. The missing letters are in the stars.

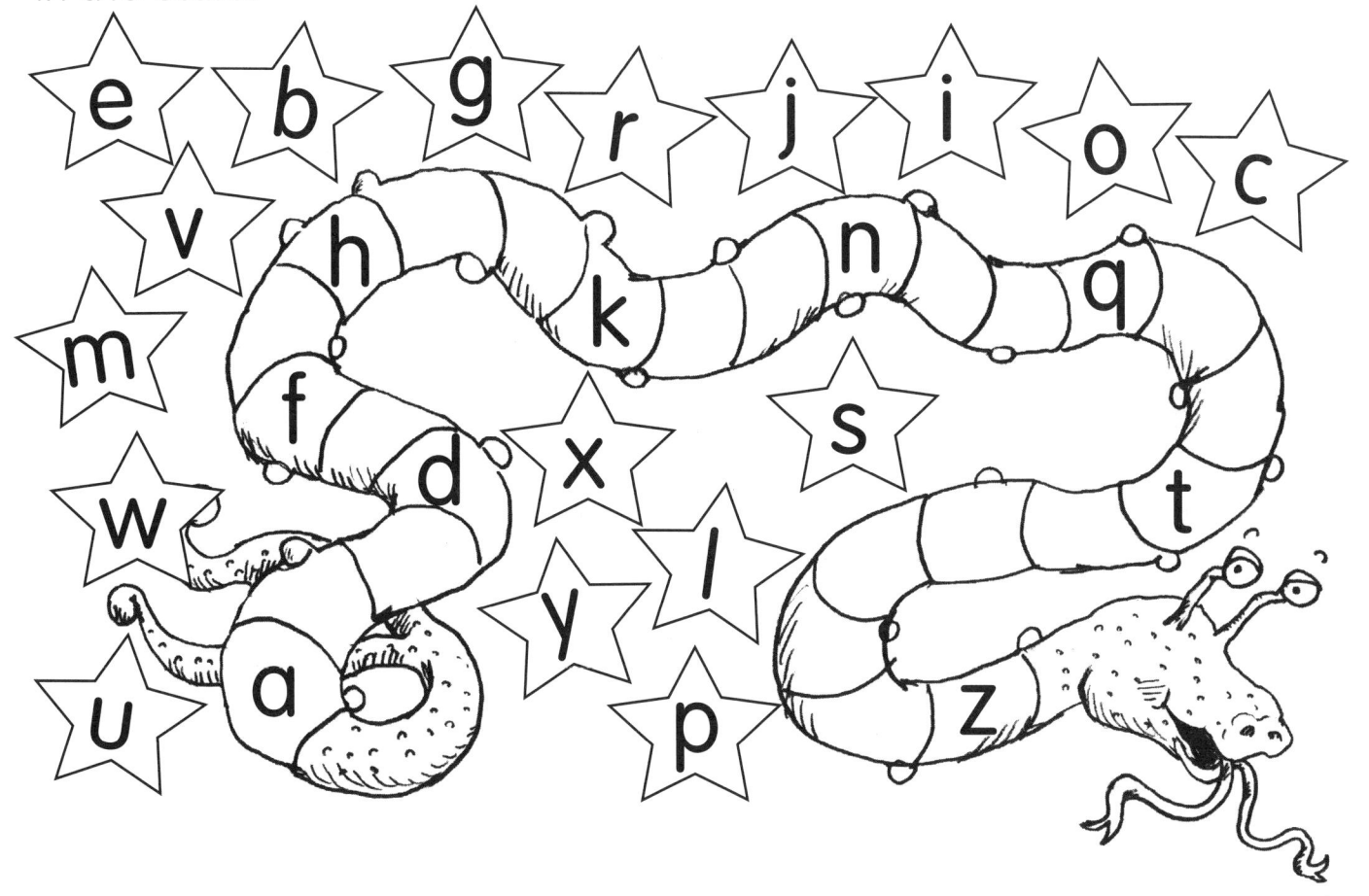

e b g r j i o c
v h n q
m k
f s
w d x t
y l
u a p z

Phonics and Spelling 2

Alphabetical order

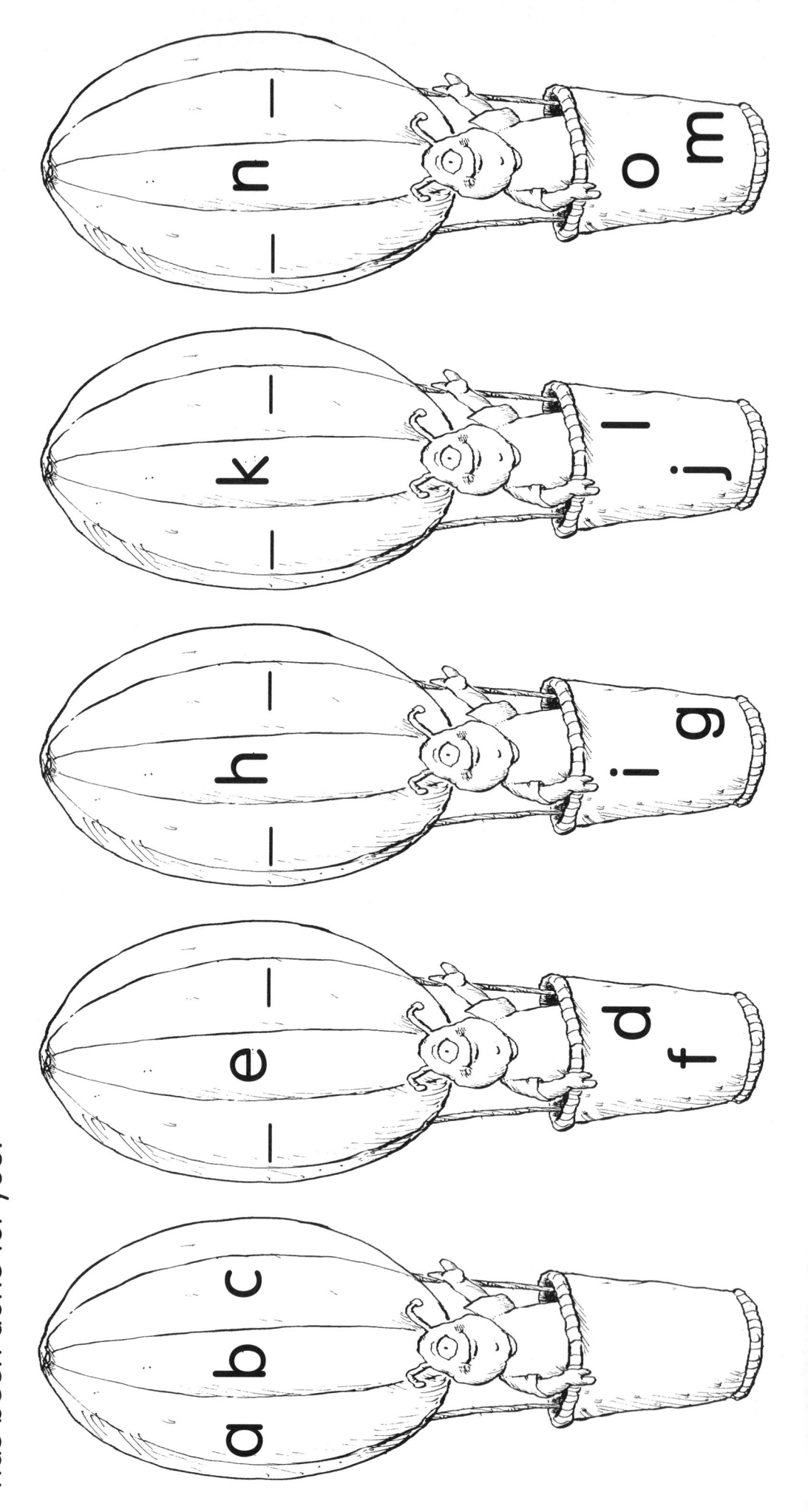

Look at the letters in each alien's hot-air balloon. Can you say each letter? Add the letters that come before and after it in the alphabet. Use the letters in the basket to help you. The first one has been done for you.

a b c
(basket: —)

_ e _
(basket: d f)

_ h _
(basket: g i)

_ k _
(basket: j l)

_ n _
(basket: m o)

Alphabetical order

Look at the letters in each alien's hot-air balloon. Can you say each letter? Add the letters that come before and after it in the alphabet. Use the letters in the basket to help you.

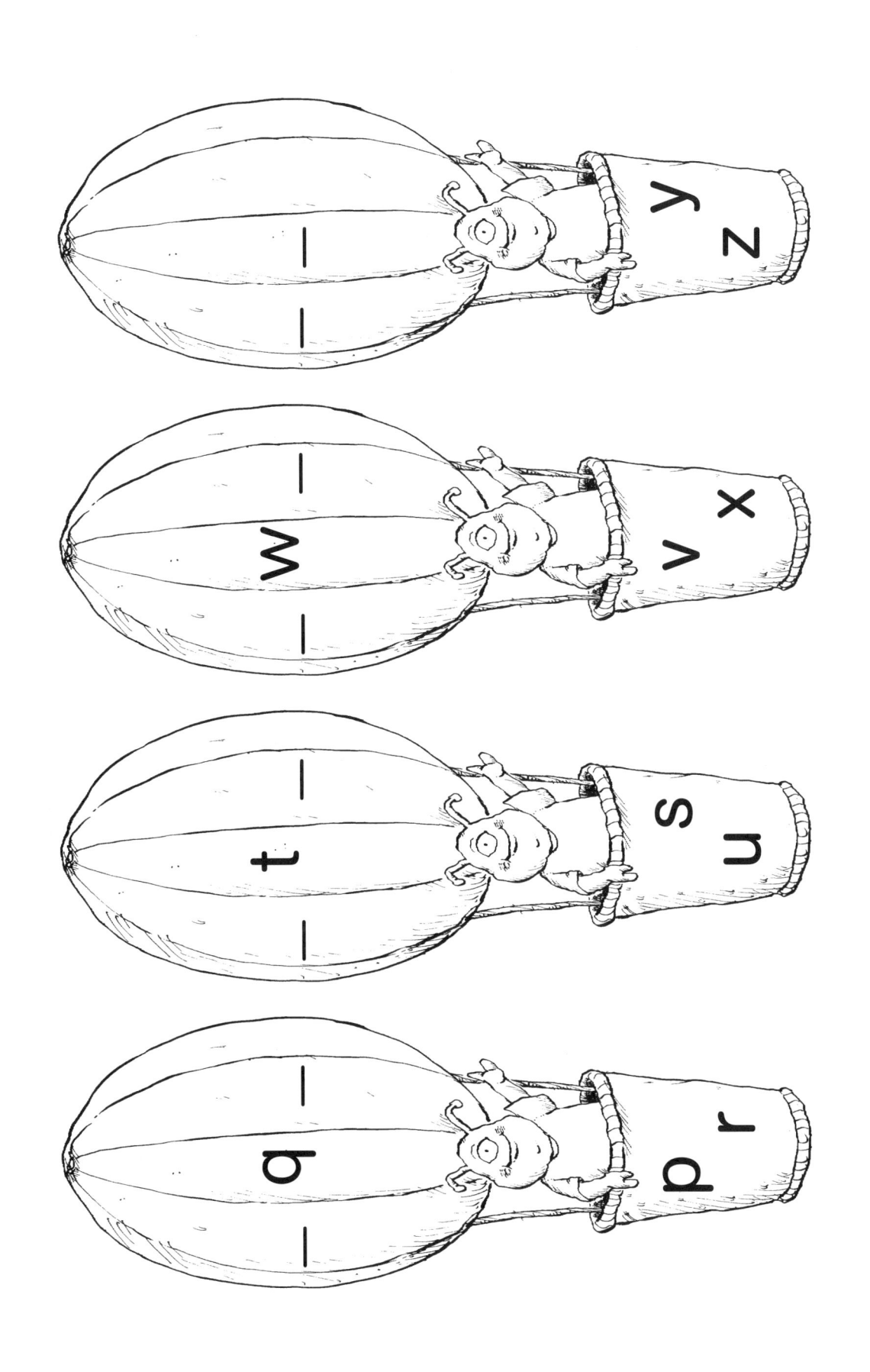

Balloon 1: _ q _
Basket: p r

Balloon 2: _ t _
Basket: s u

Balloon 3: _ w _
Basket: v x

Balloon 4: _ y _
Basket: z

Phonics and Spelling 2

Alphabetical order

What can the aliens see out of the window of their spaceship? Join the dots in alphabetical order to find out. Some letters have been joined to help you.

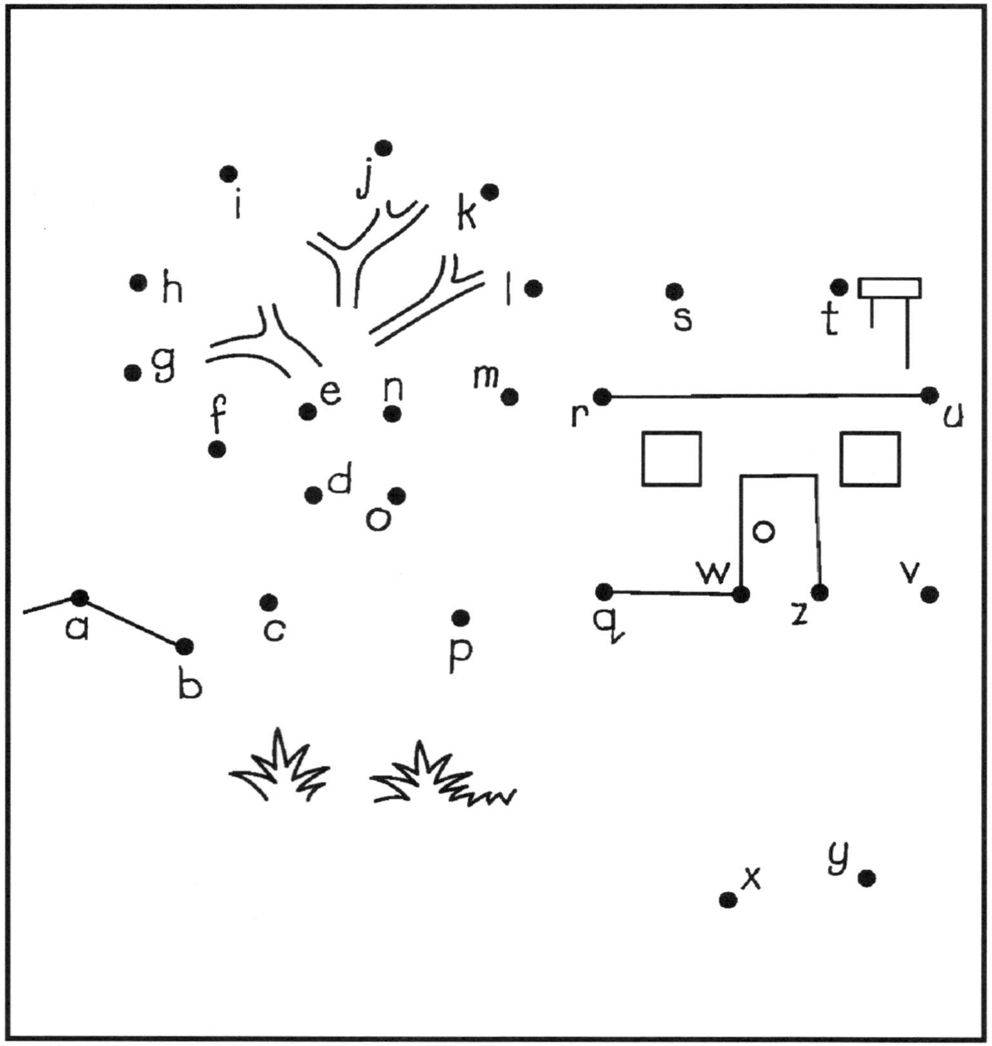

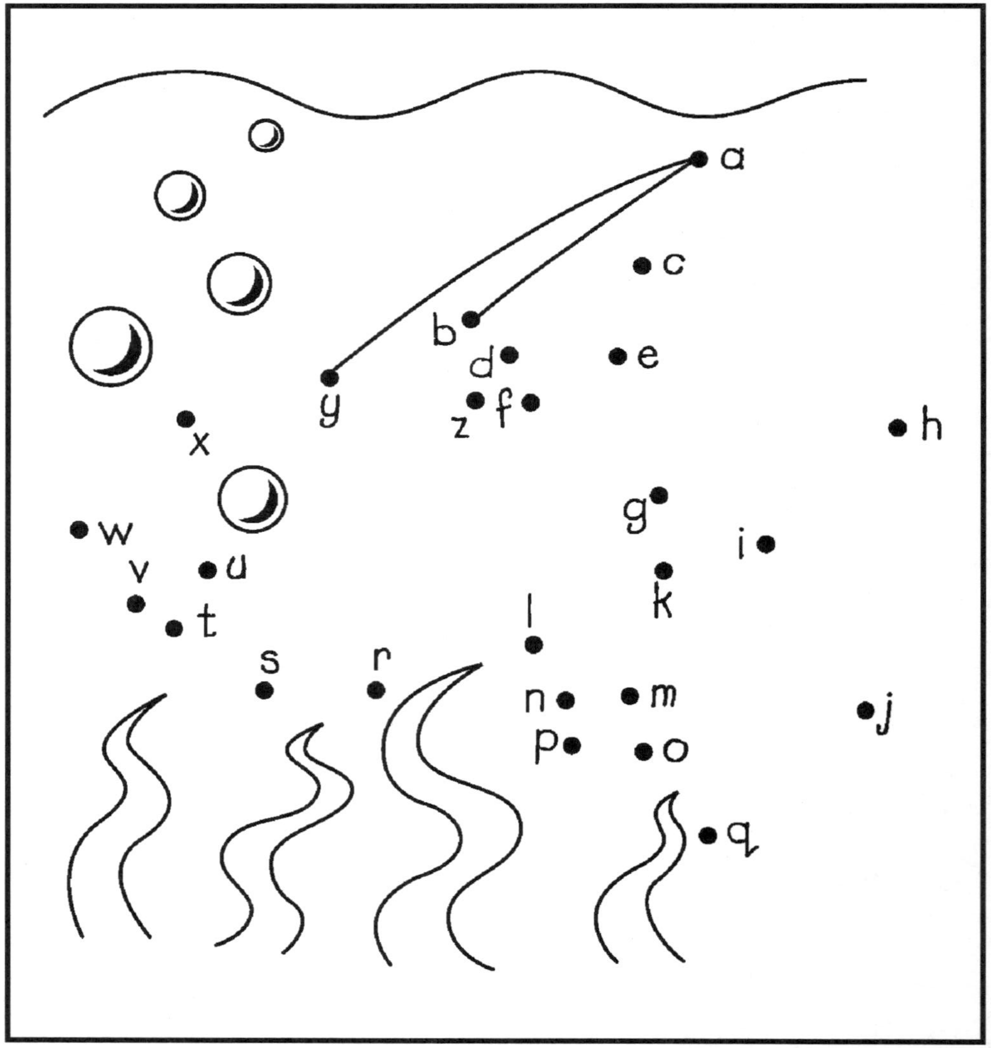

Alphabetical order

What can the aliens see out of the window of their spaceship? Join the dots in alphabetical order to find out. Some letters have been joined to help you.

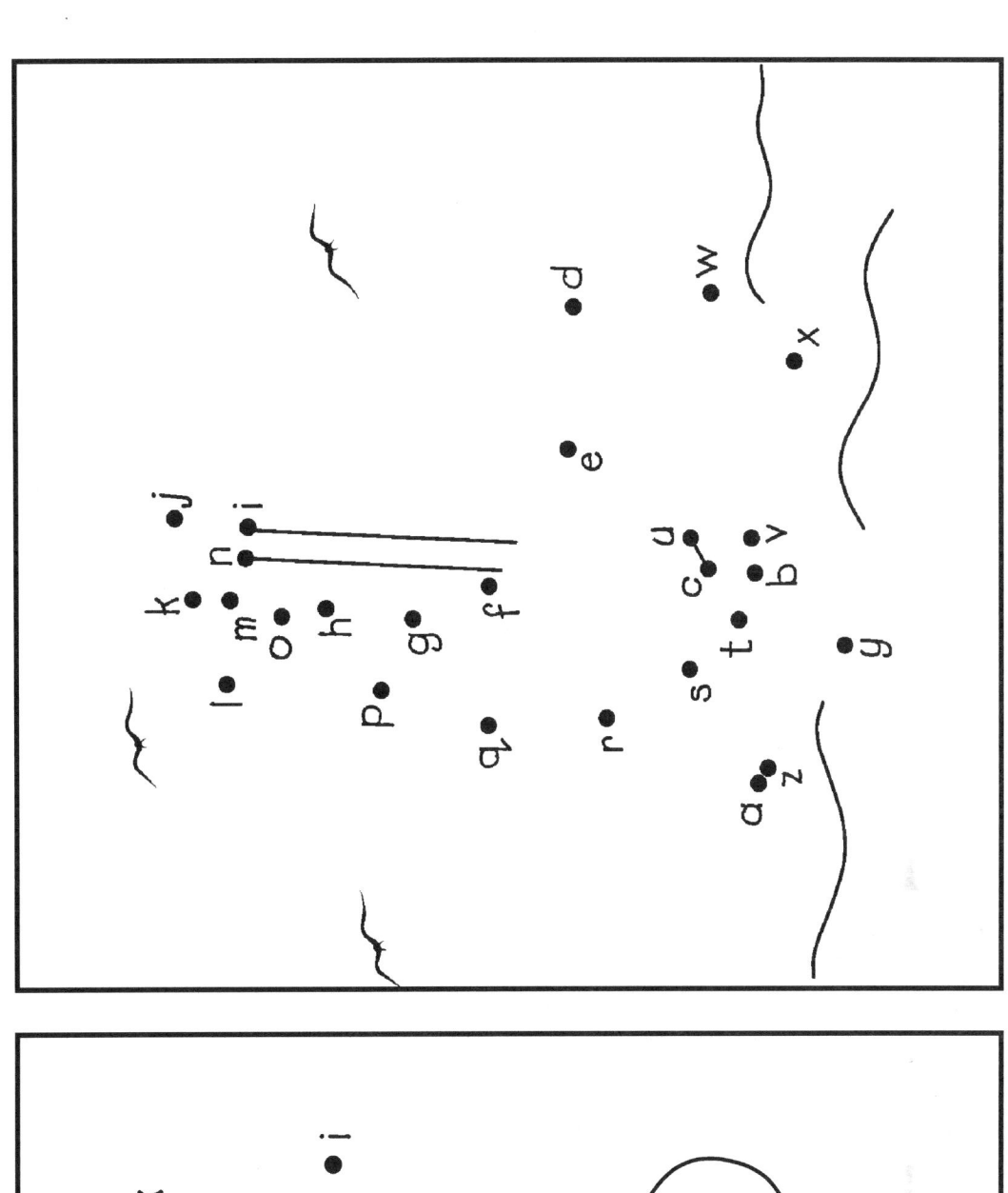

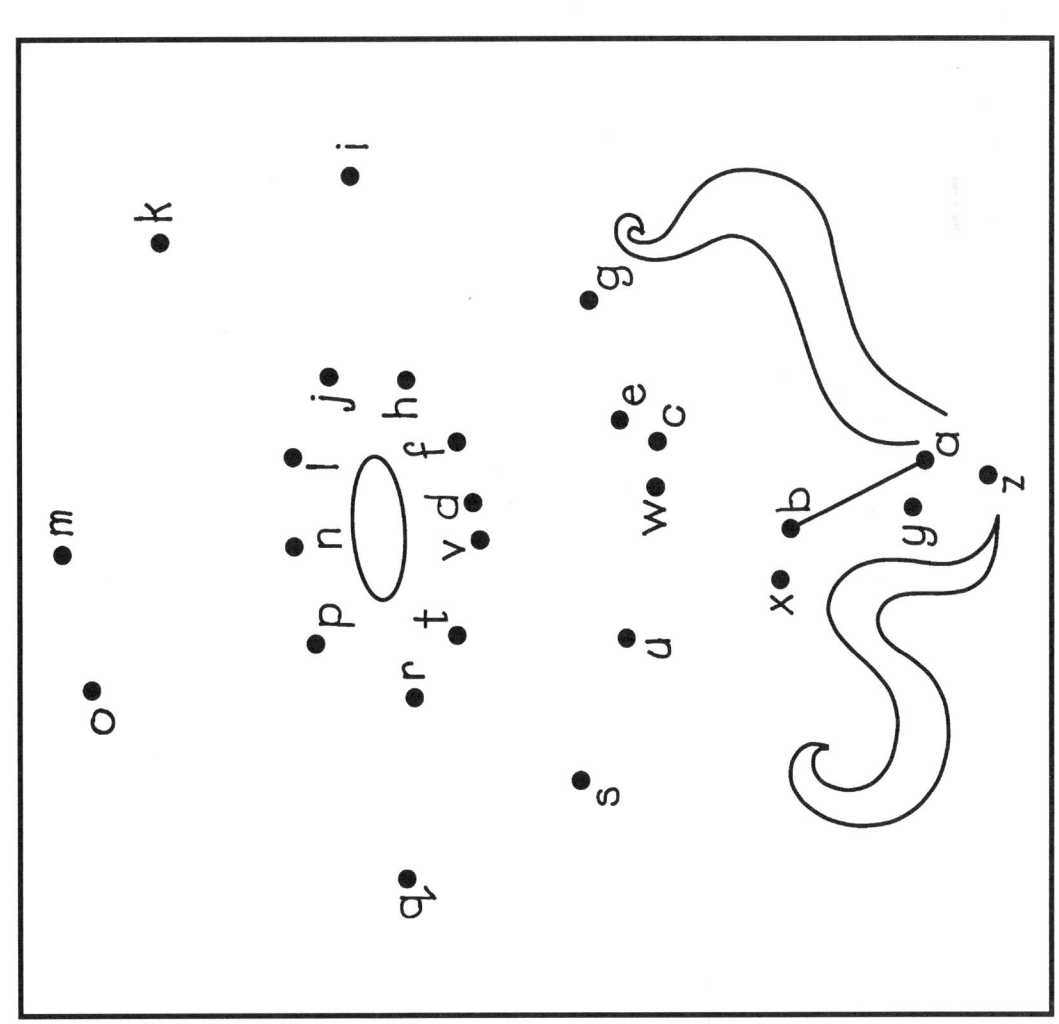

© HarperCollinsPublishers Limited 2011 Phonics and Spelling 2 13

Alphabetical order

These words and pictures are in alphabetical order from A to Z. Write the missing phonemes of the words that are next to the pictures.

ant	___ed	___at	dad	egg	___ox
gate	___en	ice	___ug	kite	___eg
___ap	nut	one	___in	queen	rib
6	___ix
___en	___mbrella	vest	___eb	x-ray	___acht
10	___ip

14   Phonics and Spelling 2   © HarperCollinsPublishers Limited 2011

Alphabetical order

These words and pictures are in alphabetical order, but the letters are jumbled up. Unjumble the letters and write the words on the lines.

apple	tba _ _ _	puc _ _ _	dad	egg	anf _ _ _
girl	ath _ _ _	ice	jam	king	leaf
omp _ _ _	ten _ _ _	oil	peg	queen	tra _ _ _
three	ugly	stev _ _ _ _	giw _ _ _	x-ray	yacht
zoo					nus _ _ _

Phonics and Spelling 2

Words that begin with bl, cl, fl, gl, pl and sl

Blend the phonemes to read the words. Join the phonemes and write the words on the lines. Cut out the pictures and stick them next to the words.

b + l + ow = _____

c + l + aw = _____

f + l + a + g = _____

g + l + ue = _____

p + l + u + g = _____

s + l + u + g = _____

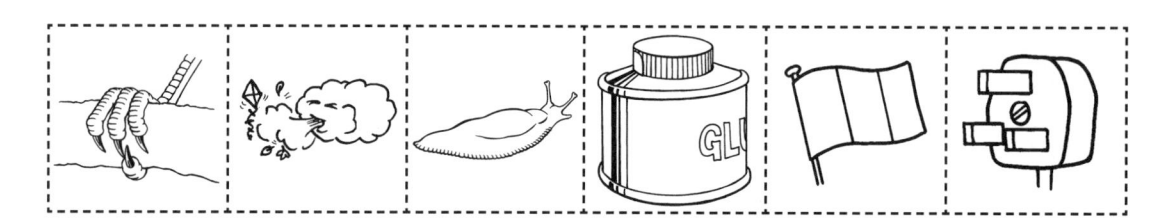

Words that begin with cr, dr, fr, gr, pr and tr

Look at the pictures and say what they show. Can you hear the phonemes in the words? Cut out the phonemes in the planets and stick them underneath the pictures to spell the words. You must use phonemes from each planet to make a word. Blend the phonemes to read the words.

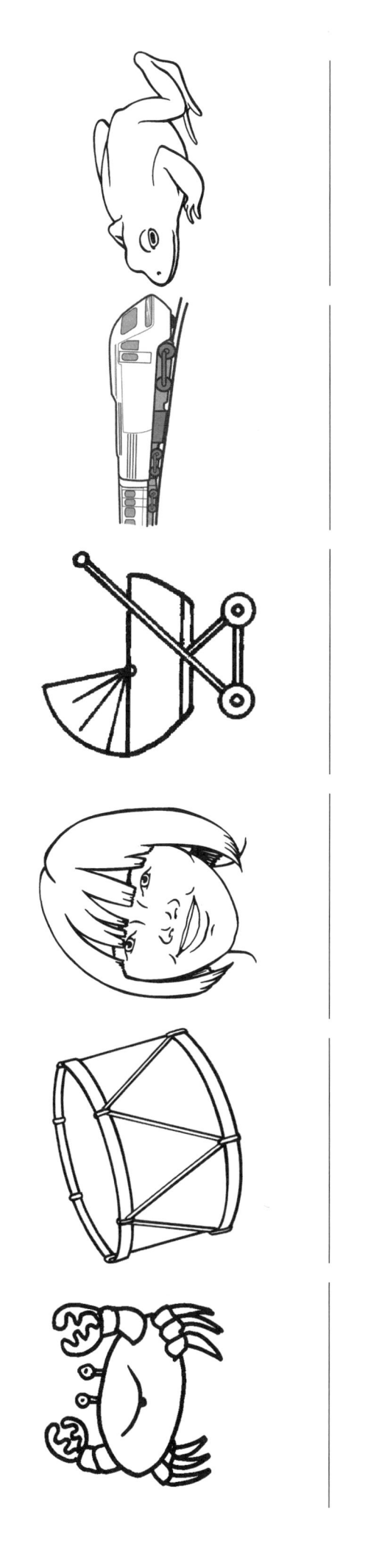

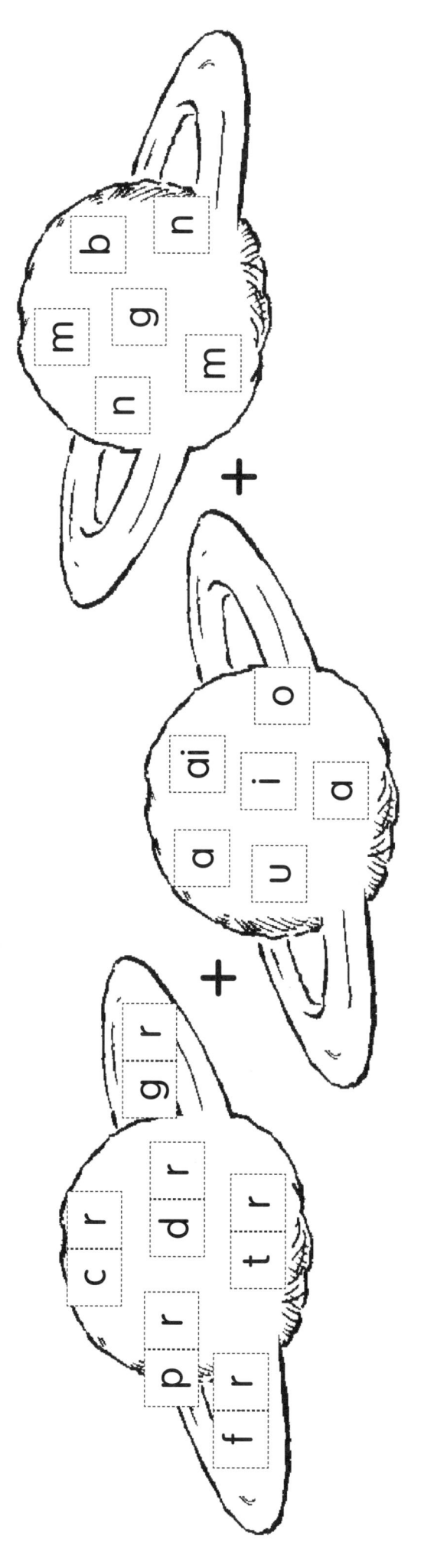

© HarperCollinsPublishers Limited 2011 Phonics and Spelling 2 17

Words that begin with dw, sw and tw

Look at the pictures and say what they are. Circle the words hidden in the wall. Join them to the pictures.

t	w	i	n	s	w	a	n
s		w		ng	d	w	ar	f
				m			
s		w	i				
t		w	e	l	ve		

12

18   Phonics and Spelling 2   © HarperCollinsPublishers Limited 2011

Words that begin with sc, sk, sm, sn, sp and st

Read the sentences. Circle the words that begin with **sc**, **sk**, **sm**, **sn**, **sp** and **st**.

★1 The cut on my leg left a bad ⟨scar⟩.
★2 I like to skip to keep fit.
★3 Some flowers smell nice.
★4 A good card game is snap.
★5 It is very rude to spit.
★6 The bus stop is next to the shop.

Look at the blends in the helmets. Write the words that you circled above on the lines next to the correct blends. One has been done for you.

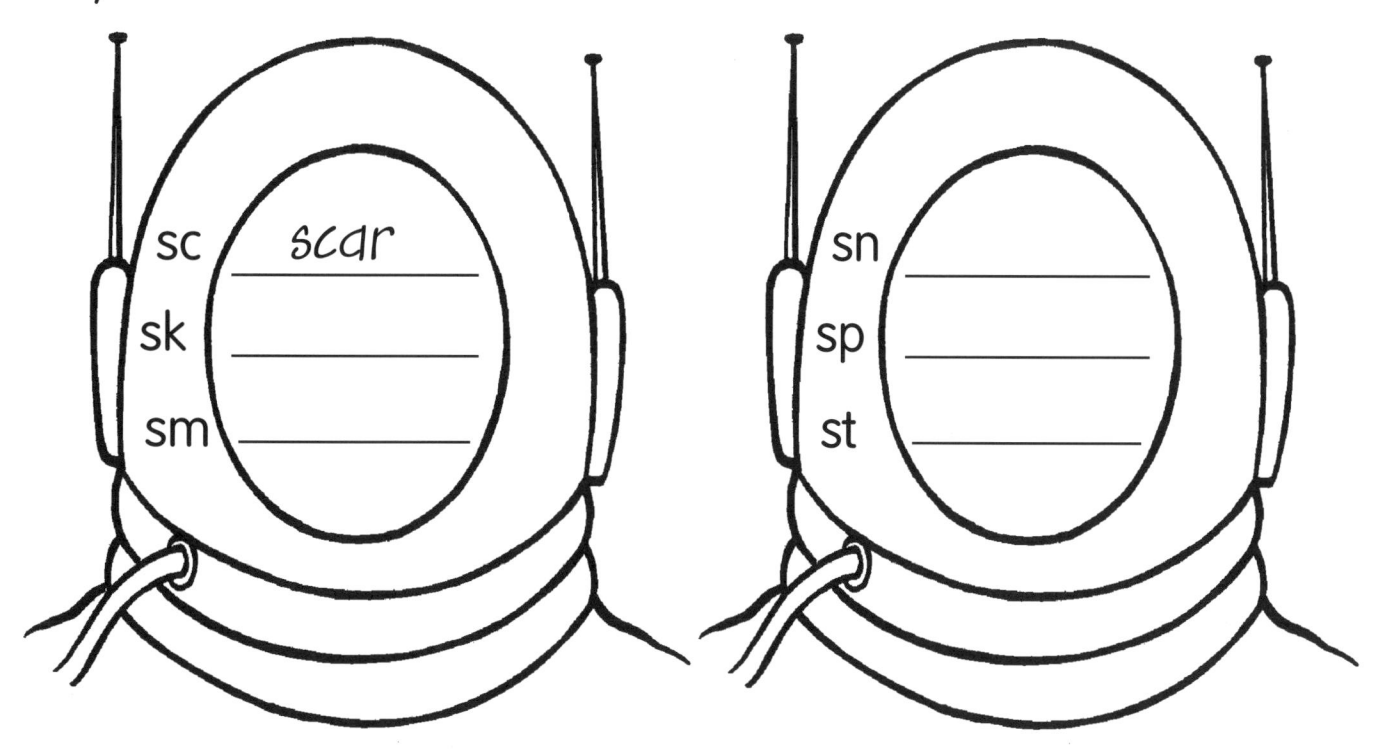

sc *scar*
sk _____
sm _____

sn _____
sp _____
st _____

Phonics and Spelling 2

Words that begin with two phonemes blended together

Read the sentences. There is a word missing from each sentence. Blend the phonemes to read the words in the boxes. Cut out the words and stick them in the correct sentences.

⭐ 1 My cut began to ☐ .

⭐ 2 Mud is ☐ .

⭐ 3 I like strawberries and ☐ .

⭐ 4 He was a funny ☐ .

⭐ 5 Catch the ball, don't ☐ it.

⭐ 6 Birds can ☐ .

⭐ 7 My painting had a red ☐ .

⭐ 8 The fire began to ☐ .

⭐ 9 My plant ☐ tall.

⭐ 10 The princess was ☐ .

| bleed |
| pretty |
| glow |
| fly |
| clown |
| frame |
| brown |
| grew |
| drop |
| cream |

Words that begin with two phonemes blended together

Blend the phonemes to read the words in the word bank. Can you hear the first two phonemes?

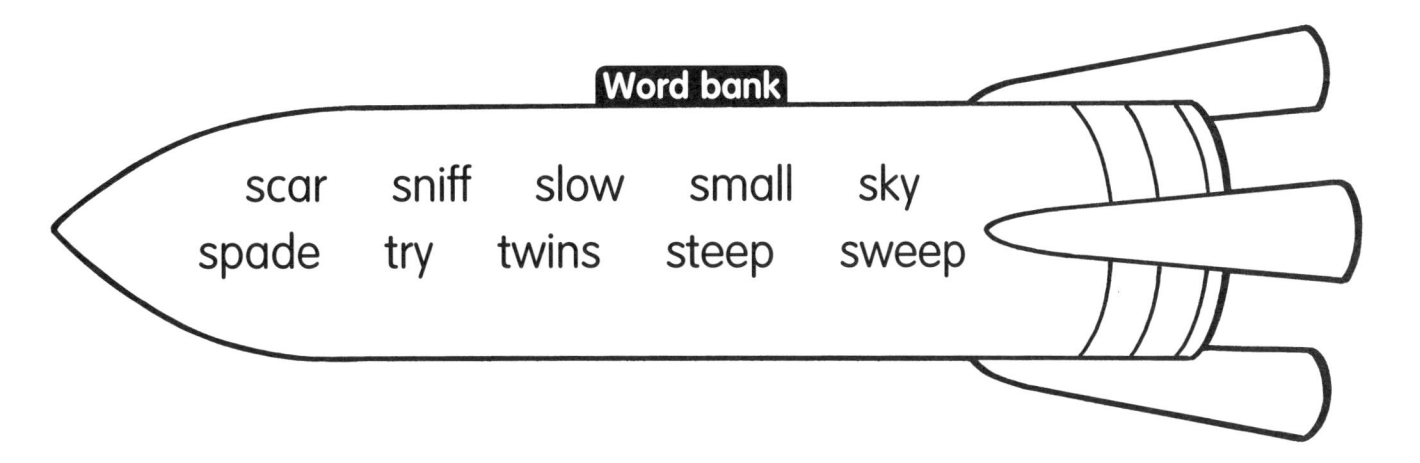

Word bank

| scar | sniff | slow | small | sky |
| spade | try | twins | steep | sweep |

Highlight the words from the word bank in the wordsearch. The words can be read across and down.

t	s	n	i	f	f	m	l
w	z	s	t	e	e	p	l
i	l	s	m	p	t	l	s
n	s	p	v	j	m	d	k
s	m	a	s	l	o	w	y
k	a	d	q	t	r	y	x
h	l	e	s	w	e	e	p
r	l	n	s	c	a	r	c

Words that begin with ch, sh and th

Blend the phonemes to read the sentences and the words in the rockets. Choose the right word to complete each sentence and write it on the line.

⭐ 1 I _____ food with my teeth.

My dog likes to _____ cats.

chase   chew

⭐ 2 I put the tins on the _____.

The _____ sells ice creams.

shelf   shop

⭐ 3 I said _____ you for the gift.

The old dog was very _____.

thank   thin

⭐ 4 After my swim, I had a hot _____.

The sun made a big _____ under the tree.

shower   shadow

⭐ 5 My _____ were red with sunburn.

Our teacher writes with _____.

chalk   cheeks

Words that begin with scr and spl

Blend the phonemes to read the letter strings in the rockets. Join the parts together and write them on the lines. The first one has been done for you.

screen

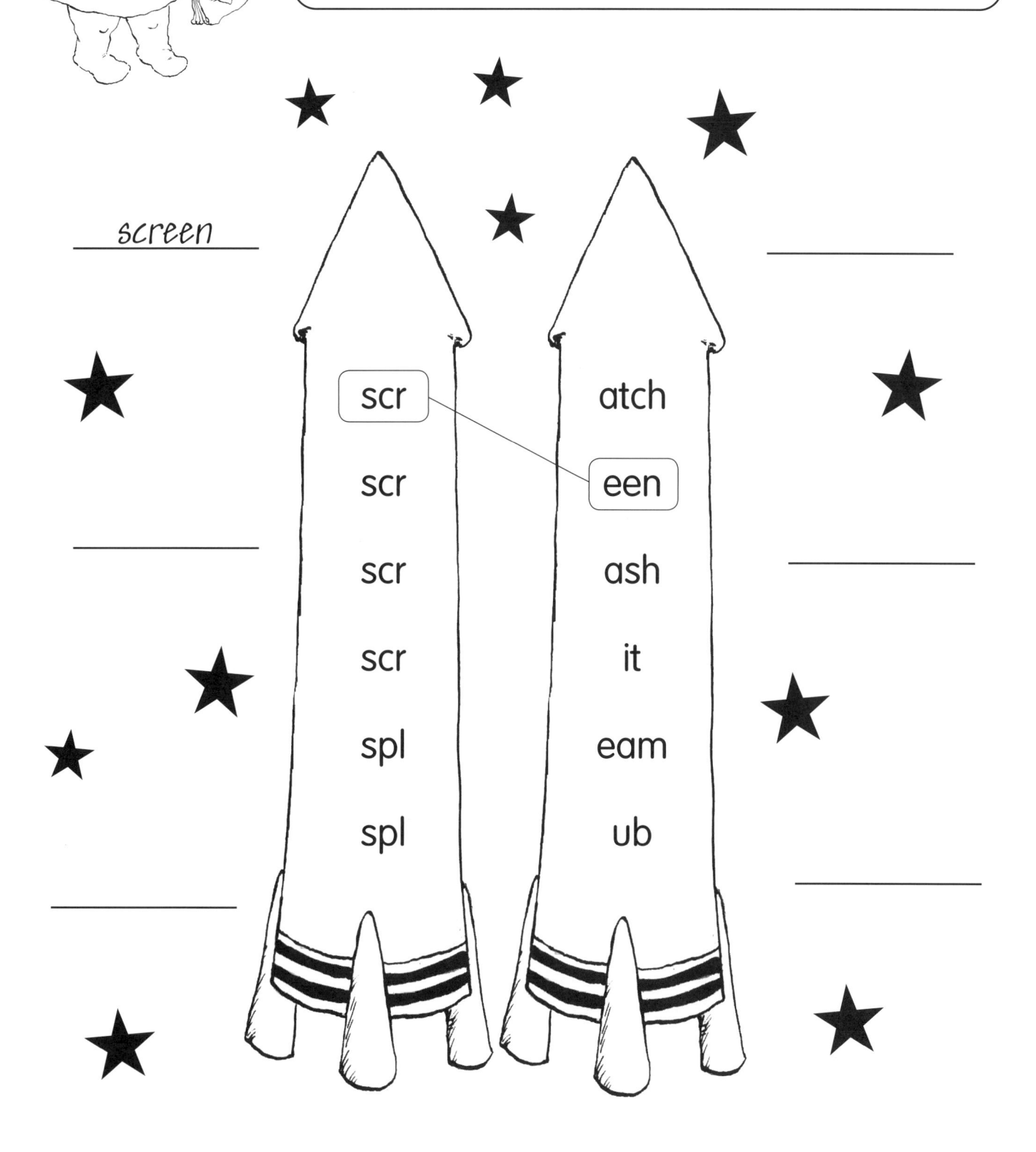

scr	atch
scr	een
scr	ash
scr	it
spl	eam
spl	ub

Words that begin with spr and squ

Look at the pictures in the balloons and say what they show. Blend the letter strings in the feet of the aliens to read the words. Write the words in the aliens. Join the aliens to the correct balloons.

spr | ing   squ | are   spr | ay   squ | irt

Words that begin with str

Look at the pictures and say what they show. The phonemes in the words are jumbled up. Sort them out and write them in the boxes. Each word begins with **str**.

t s r aw

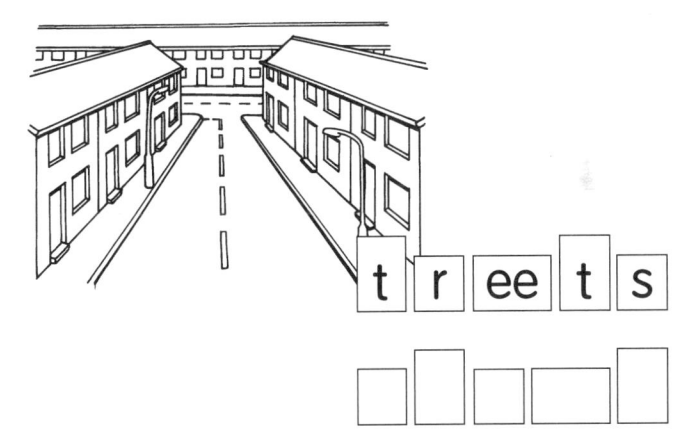

t r ee t s

i r t n g s

t r n g s o

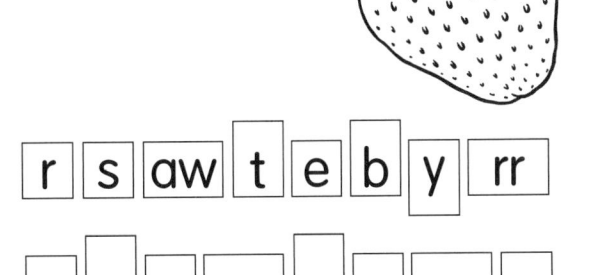

r s aw t e b y rr

s e t r t ch

Words that begin with scr, spl, spr and str

Look at the pictures and say what they are or what action they show. Can you hear the blend at the start of the word? Choose the missing blend from the footprints and write it in the boxes in the rockets. Write the words on the lines.

scr   spl   spr   str

1. ☐☐☐ew _____
2. ☐☐☐ash _____
3. ☐☐☐ub _____
4. ☐☐☐ing _____
5. ☐☐☐int _____
6. ☐☐☐ing _____

Phonics and Spelling 2

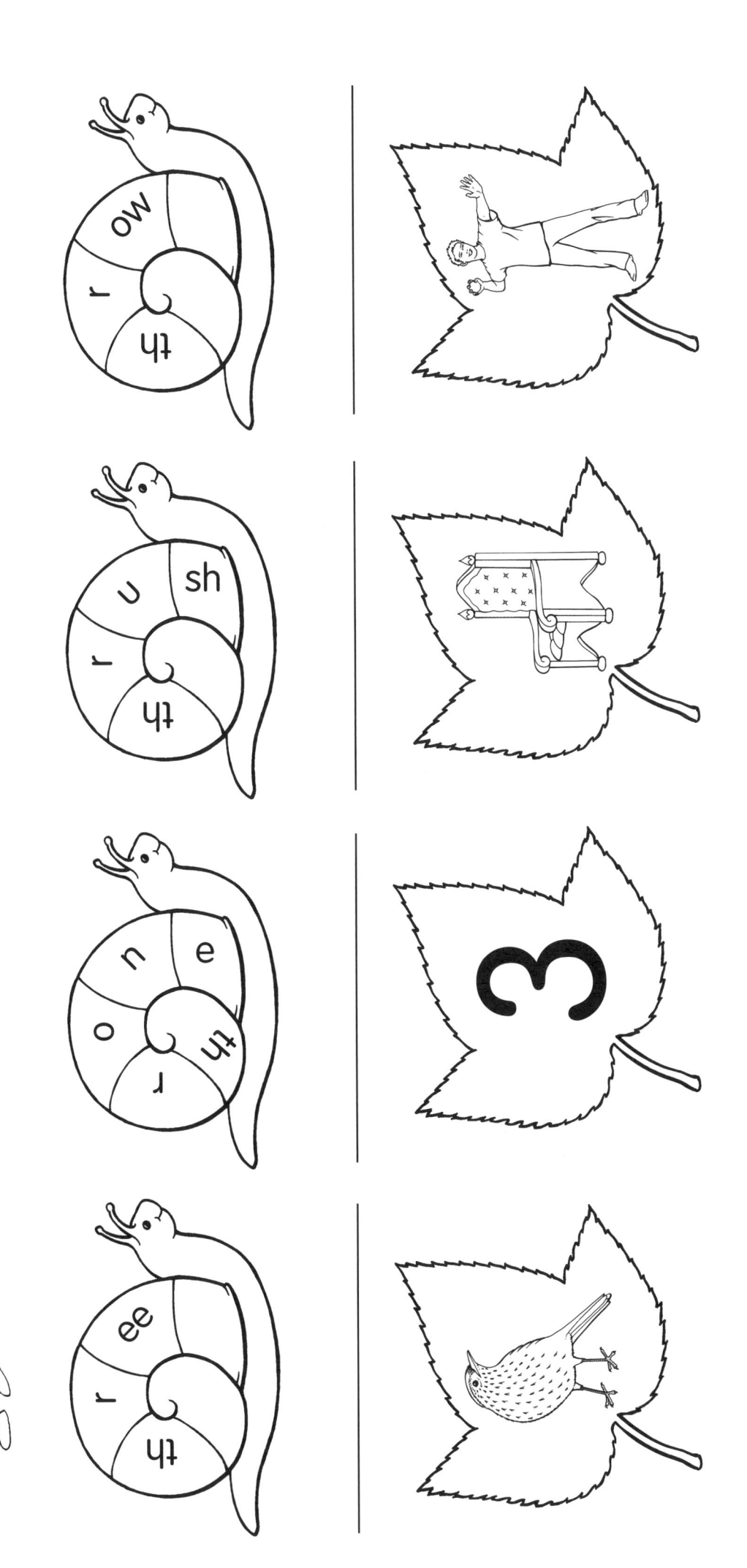

Words that begin with thr

Look at the pictures in the leaves and say what they show. The phonemes in each snails' shells spell the words. Write them on the lines and join each snail to the right picture.

Phonics and Spelling 2

Words that begin with thr and shr

Blend the phonemes to read the words. Break the words up into phonemes like the example. Remember, some phonemes, such as **th** and **sh**, are spelt with more than one letter.

Example: throat → | th | r | oa | t |

thrill →

thrush →

throw →

three →

shrub →

shriek →

shrug →

shrink →

3

28   Phonics and Spelling 2   © HarperCollinsPublishers Limited 2011

Words that begin with scr, spl, spr, squ, str and thr

Blend the phonemes to read the letter strings in the planets. Now read the sentences below. Add a letter string from the planets to complete the missing word in each sentence. The first one has been done for you.

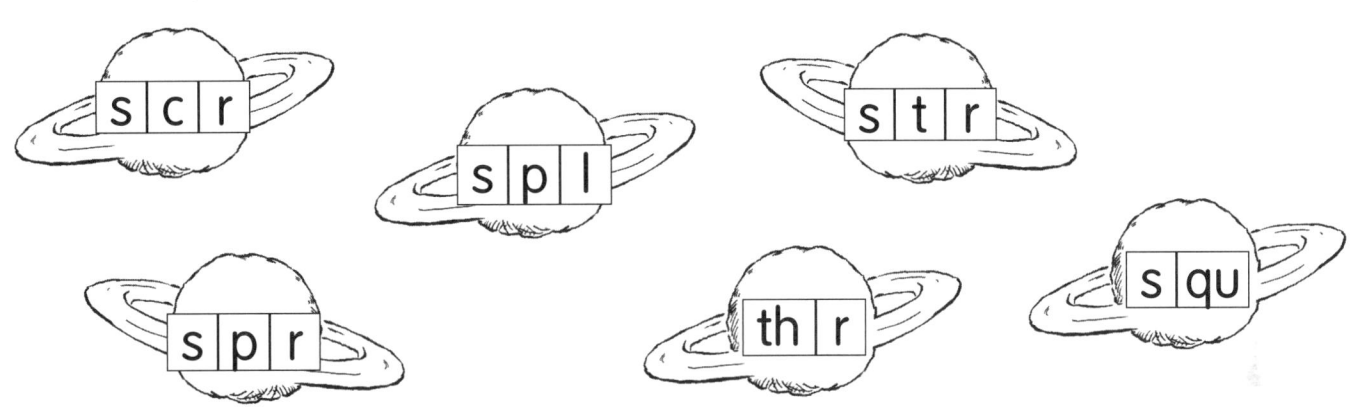

[scr] [spl] [str] [spr] [thr] [squ]

★1 I had a small [s][c][r][a][p] of paper to write my name on.

★2 The [ ][ ][a][y] dog had no home.

★3 We had to [ ][ ][a][s][h] the clothes into the small case.

★4 The fish were in the [ ][ ][ea][m].

★5 I had to [ ][ ][ea][d] the needle to sew.

★6 I [ ][ ][ew] the ball into the net.

★7 He had a [ ][ ][i][n][t][er] of wood in his finger.

★8 She jumps up and down as if she is on [ ][ ][i][n][g][s].

★9 I [ ][ ][ea][d] the jam on my toast.

★10 The mouse made my mum [ ][ ][ea][m].

★★★★★★★★★★★

The blends ch, ph and wh

Look at the pictures and read the words to say what they are.

Christmas    photo 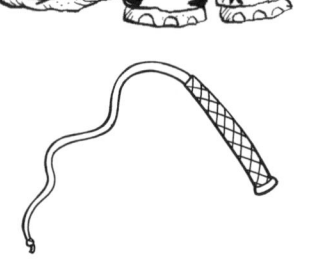   whip

Can you hear the phonemes at the start? Look at the way they are spelt.

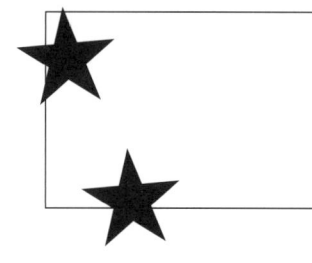

ch says **c** or **k**   **ph** says **f**

wh says **w**

Blend the phonemes to read the words below. Find and circle the **ch**, **ph** or **wh** in these words.

white   elephant   when

chorus   whip   wheel

whale   photo   telephone

Words that rhyme

Blend the phonemes to read the words on the planets. Some of these words rhyme. Help the aliens get back to their spaceships. Colour the words that rhyme with the shaded word to show them the way.

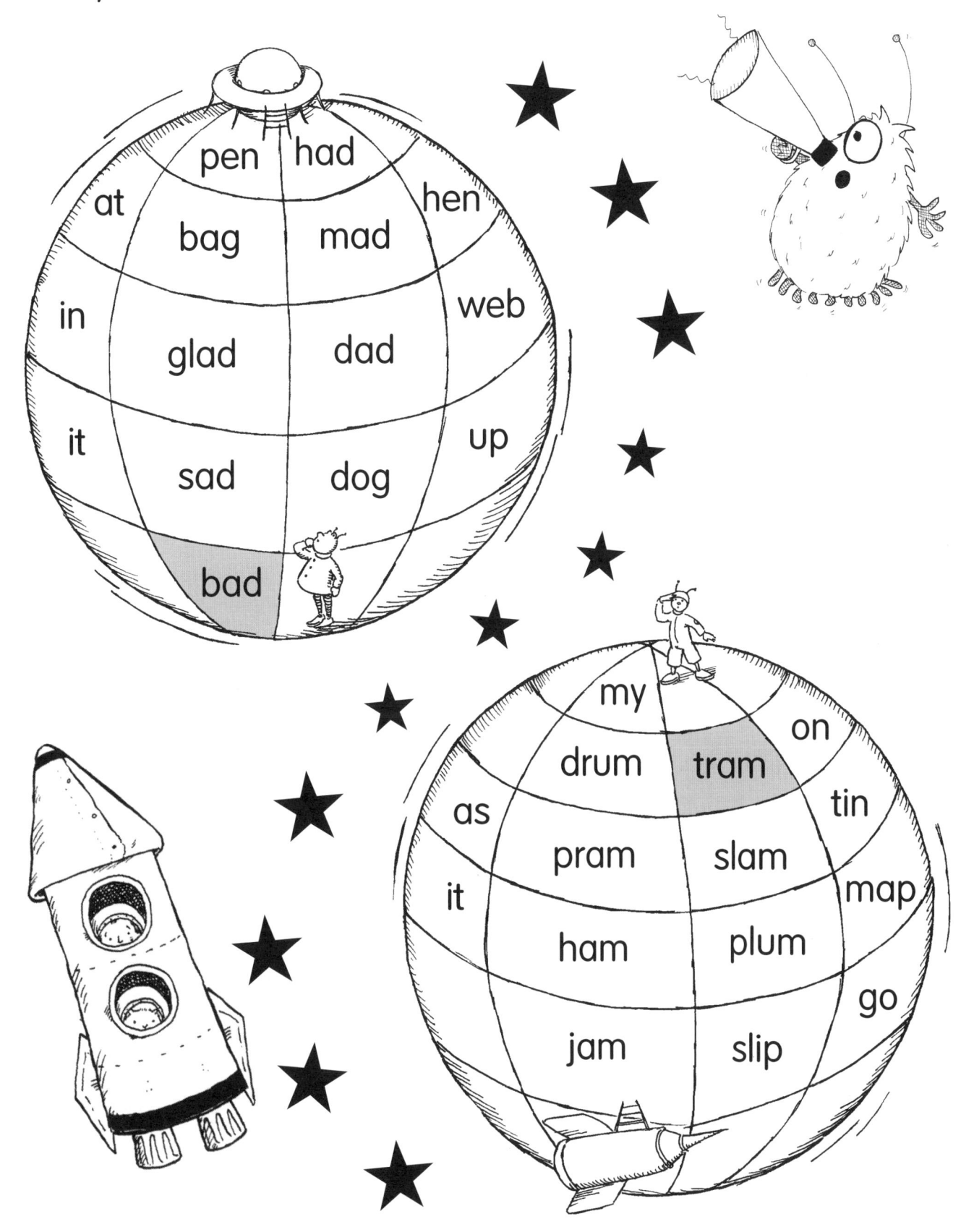

Planet 1 (shaded word: **bad**):
pen, had, at, hen, bag, mad, in, web, glad, dad, it, up, sad, dog, bad

Planet 2 (shaded word: **tram**):
my, on, drum, tram, as, tin, pram, slam, it, map, ham, plum, go, jam, slip

Words that rhyme

Blend the phonemes to read the words. Can you hear the words with the same middle and end phonemes? These words rhyme. Colour the words that rhyme in each group.

can
nut
plan
fan

clap
rip cap
trap

hat
cat flag bat

Words that rhyme

Blend the phonemes to read the words in the rockets. Can you hear the words with the same middle and end phonemes? These words rhyme. Join the words that rhyme from left to right. The first two words have been joined for you.

10

red	ten	shed	fed
hen	bed	men	peg
leg	beg	keg	pen

Phonics and Spelling 2

Words that rhyme

Words that rhyme have the same middle and end phonemes. For example:

| h | a | t | and | c | a | t | ★ | d | o | g | and | l | o | g |

Use a phoneme from each rocket with the i in the planet to make words that rhyme with the blends in the stars. Write the words on the lines.

Rocket 1: b, p, n, s, h — star: ip

Planet: i — star: in

Rocket 2: n, p, t — star: it

Words that rhyme

Look at the pictures and say what they show. Can you hear the words with the same middle and end phonemes? These are words that rhyme. Write the first phoneme of each word. Join those that rhyme to the stars in the middle.

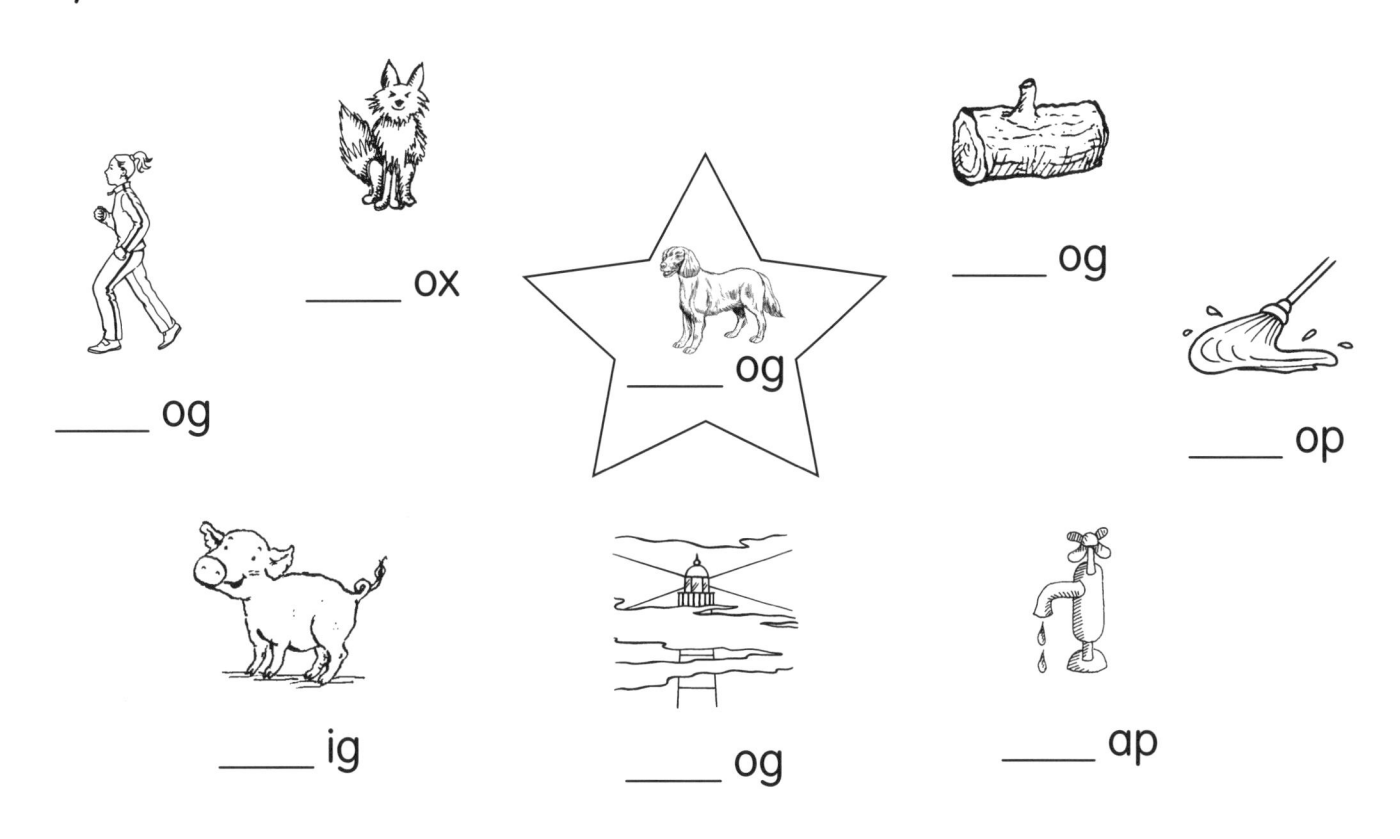

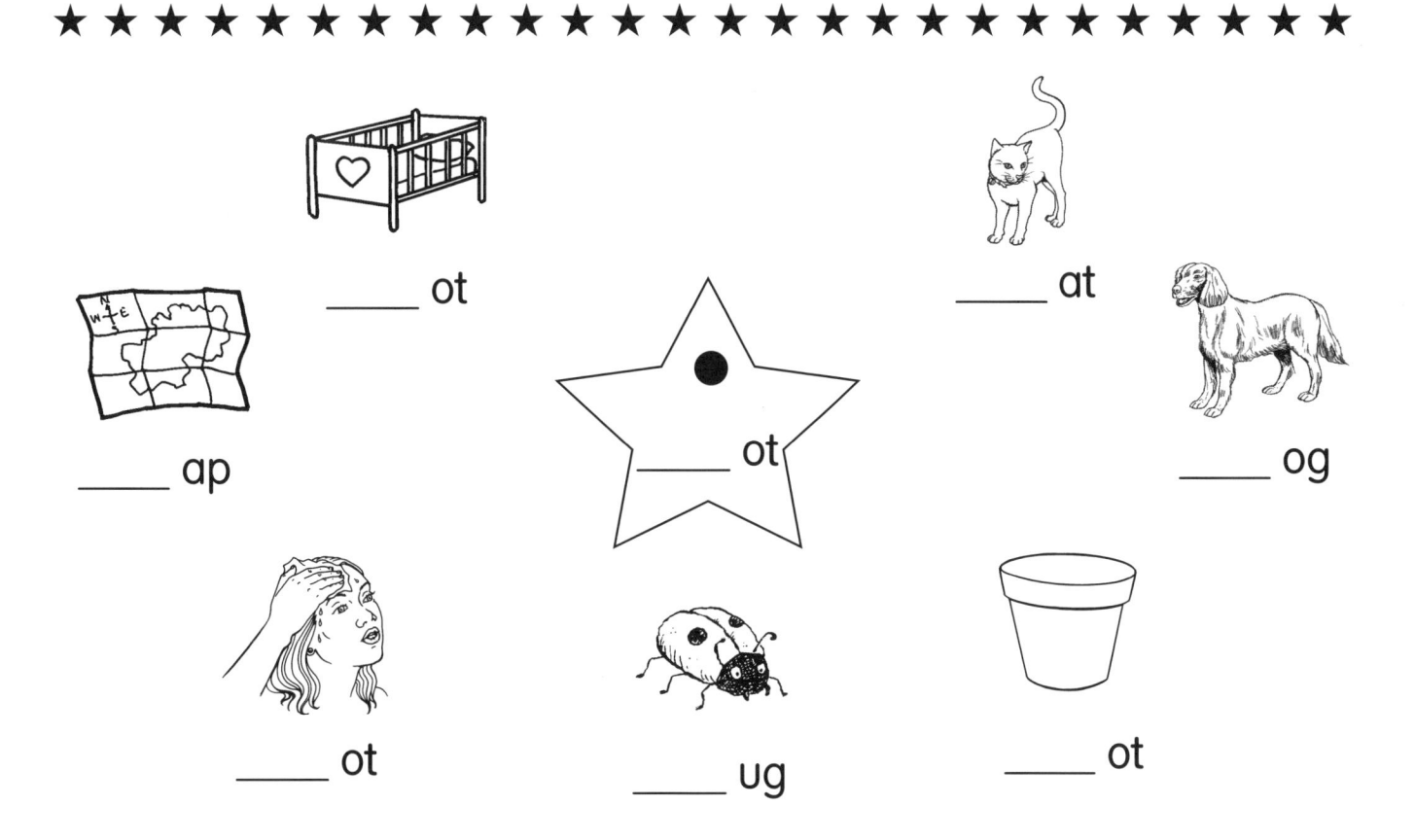

___ og   ___ ox   ___ og (star)   ___ og   ___ op

___ ig   ___ og   ___ ap

★★★★★★★★★★★★★★★★★★★★★★★★★★★★★

___ ot   ___ at

___ ap   ___ ot (star)   ___ og

___ ot   ___ ug   ___ ot

Phonics and Spelling 2

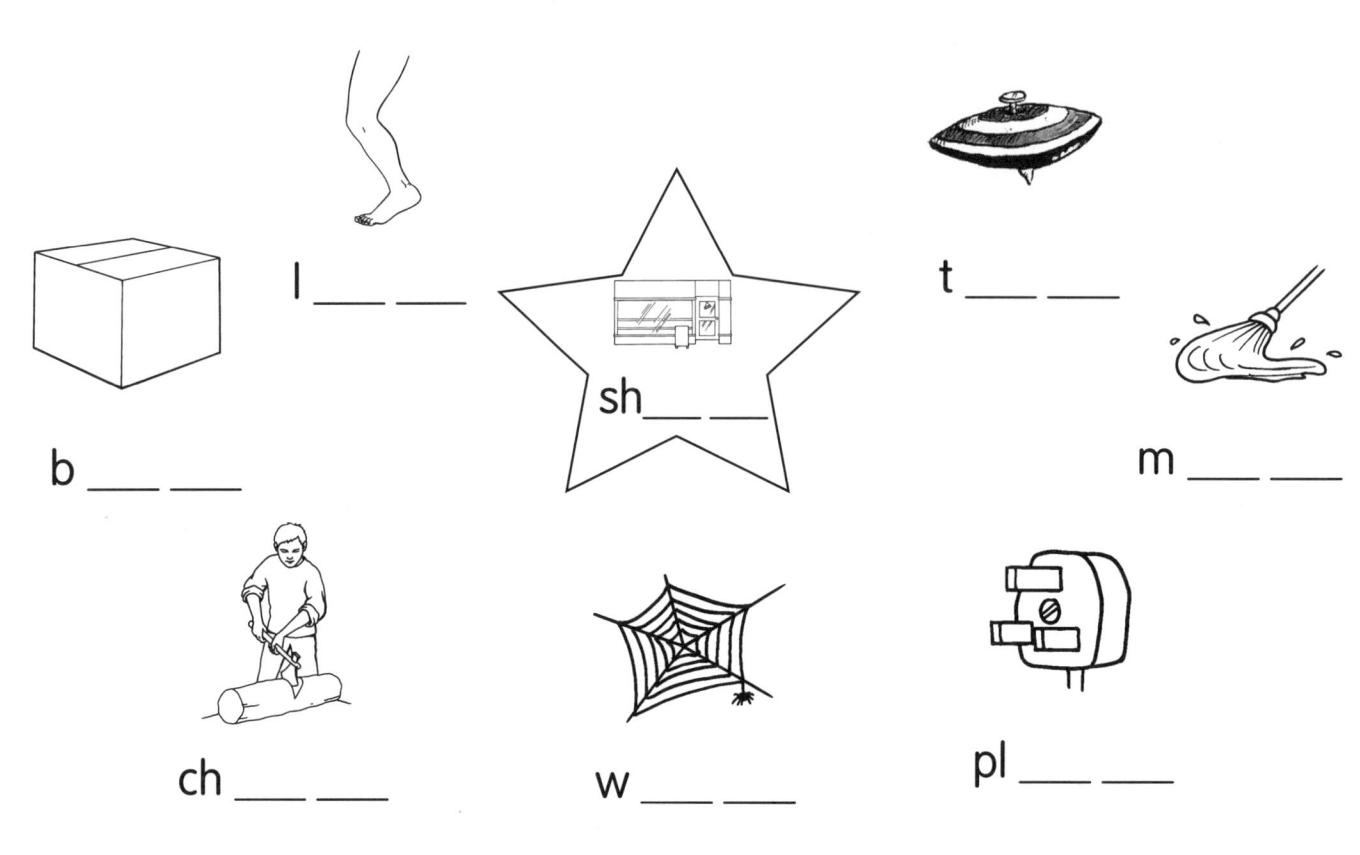

Words that rhyme

Write in the middle and end phonemes. Blend the phonemes and say the words. Circle the pictures that rhyme with the word in the star.

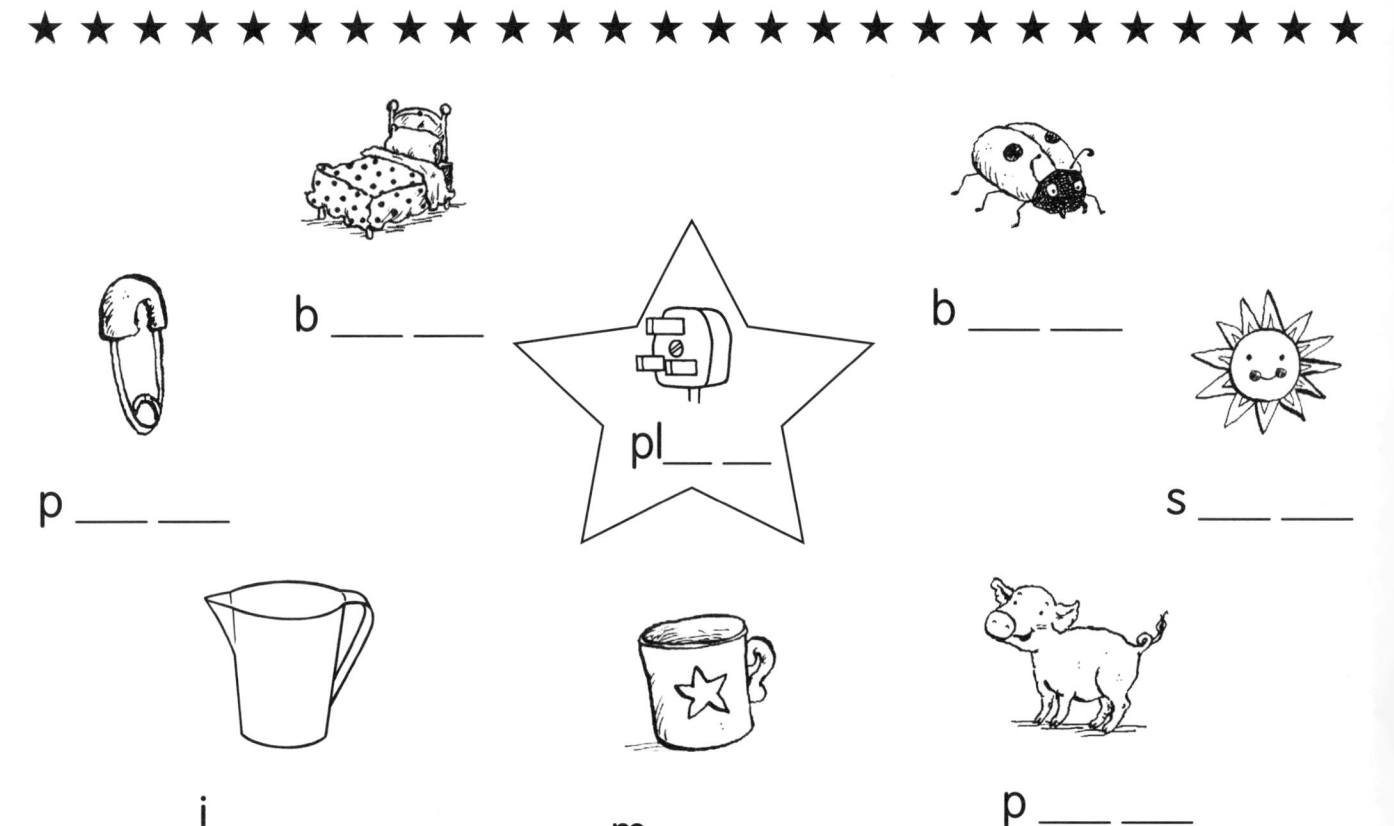

b ___ ___   l ___ ___   sh ___ ___   t ___ ___   m ___ ___

ch ___ ___   w ___ ___   pl ___ ___

★ ★

p ___ ___   b ___ ___   pl ___ ___   b ___ ___   s ___ ___

j ___ ___   m ___ ___   p ___ ___

Phonics and Spelling 2

Words that rhyme

Look at the pictures in the stars and read the word. Can you hear the middle and end phonemes? Cut out the words at the bottom of the page. Stick the words with the same middle and end phonemes in the spaceships next to the pictures.

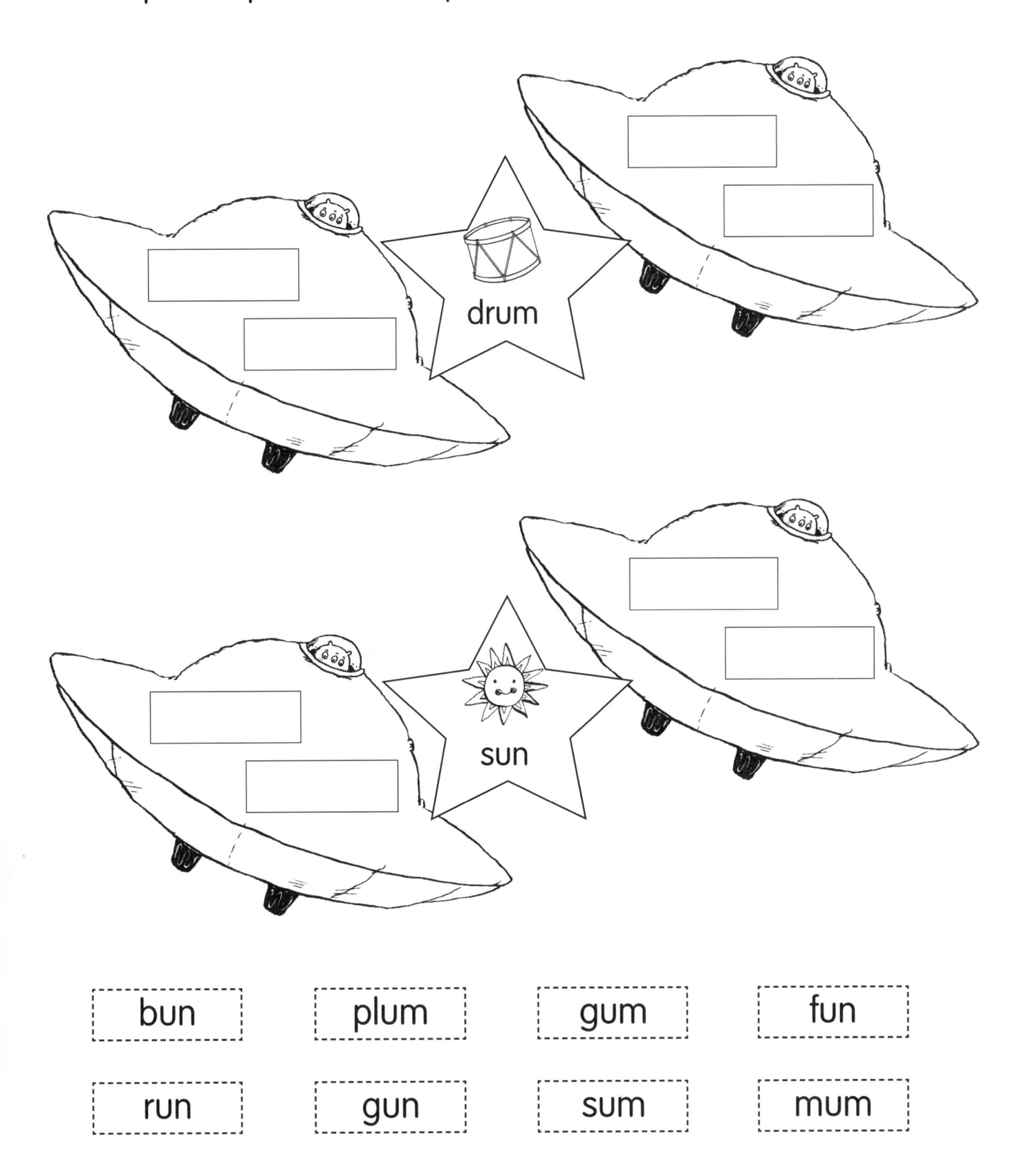

drum

sun

| bun | plum | gum | fun |
| run | gun | sum | mum |

Phonics and Spelling 2

Words that end in ld, nd and rd

Look at the pictures and say what they show. Blend the phonemes and say the words. Can you hear the phonemes at the ends of the words? Circle the correct word for each picture. Some of them are not real words.

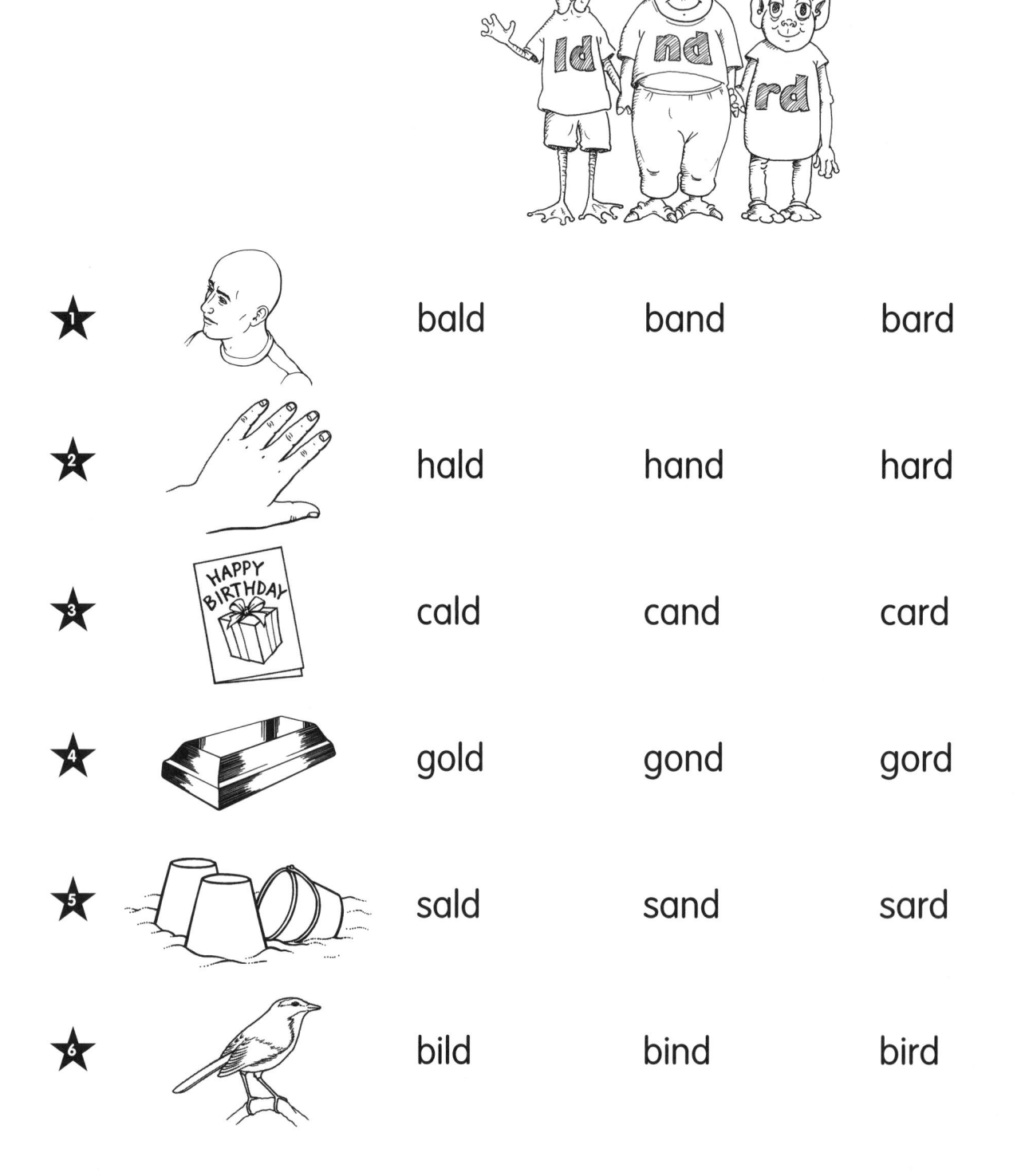

		bald	band	bard
★ 1				
★ 2		hald	hand	hard
★ 3		cald	cand	card
★ 4		gold	gond	gord
★ 5		sald	sand	sard
★ 6		bild	bind	bird

Words that end in lk, nk and rk

Blend the phonemes to read the words at the bottom of the page. Look at the pictures and say what they show. Cut out the words and stick them by the pictures. One has been done for you.

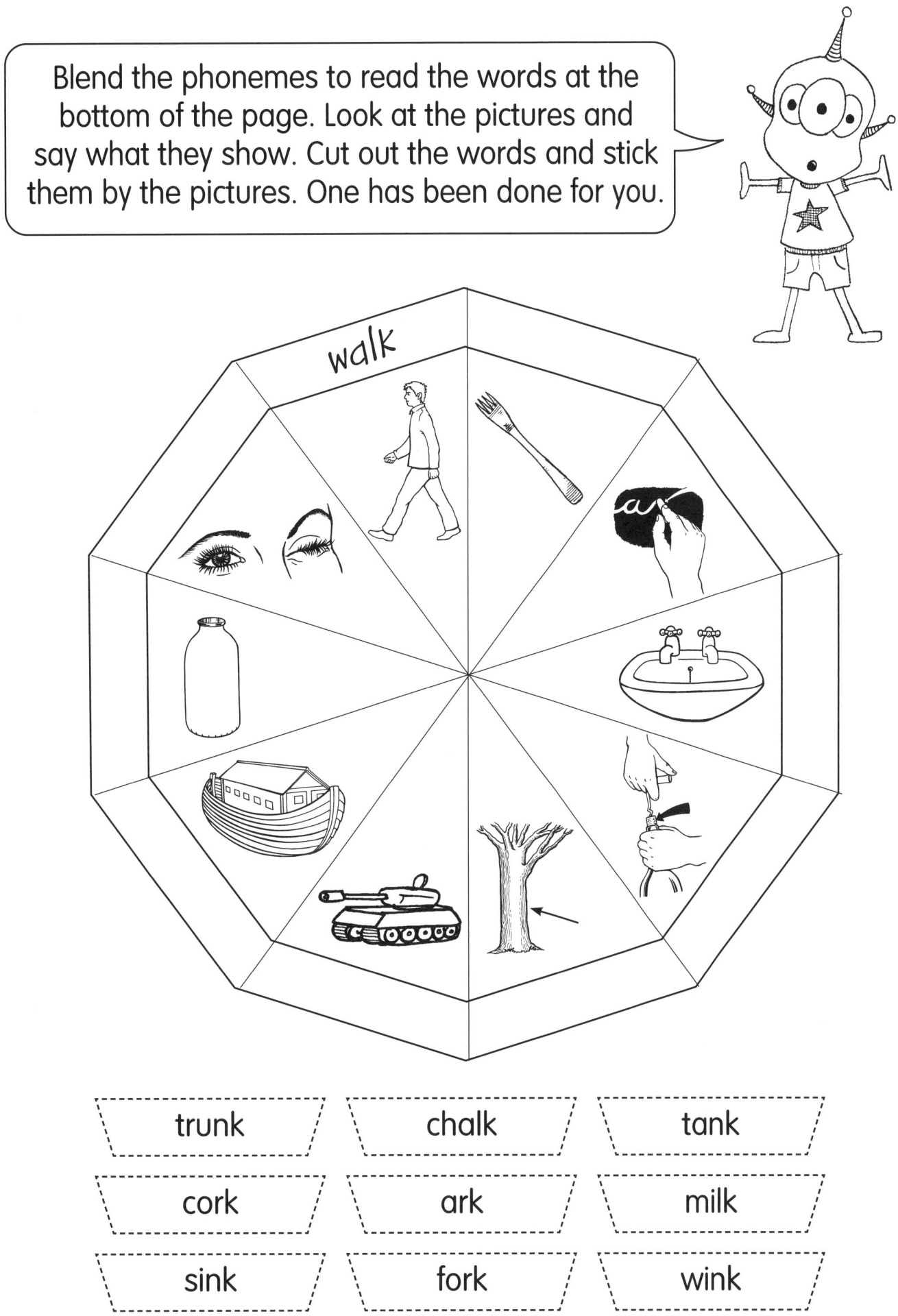

walk

trunk	chalk	tank
cork	ark	milk
sink	fork	wink

Words that end in lm and rm

Blend the phonemes and read the sentences. Say the words in the boxes at the bottom of the page. Cut out the words and stick them in the correct sentences.

★ 1 There was no wind and the sea was ☐ .

★ 2 On the island there were lots of ☐ trees.

★ 3 Cows and sheep are ☐ animals.

★ 4 The fire ☐ went off when I burnt my toast.

★ 5 The boat sank in the ☐ .

★ 6 A movie is the same as a ☐ .

| film | alarm | calm | palm | storm | farm |

Words that end in lp, mp, rp and sp

Blend the phonemes to read the words in the rockets. Write the words in the spaceships so that they rhyme.

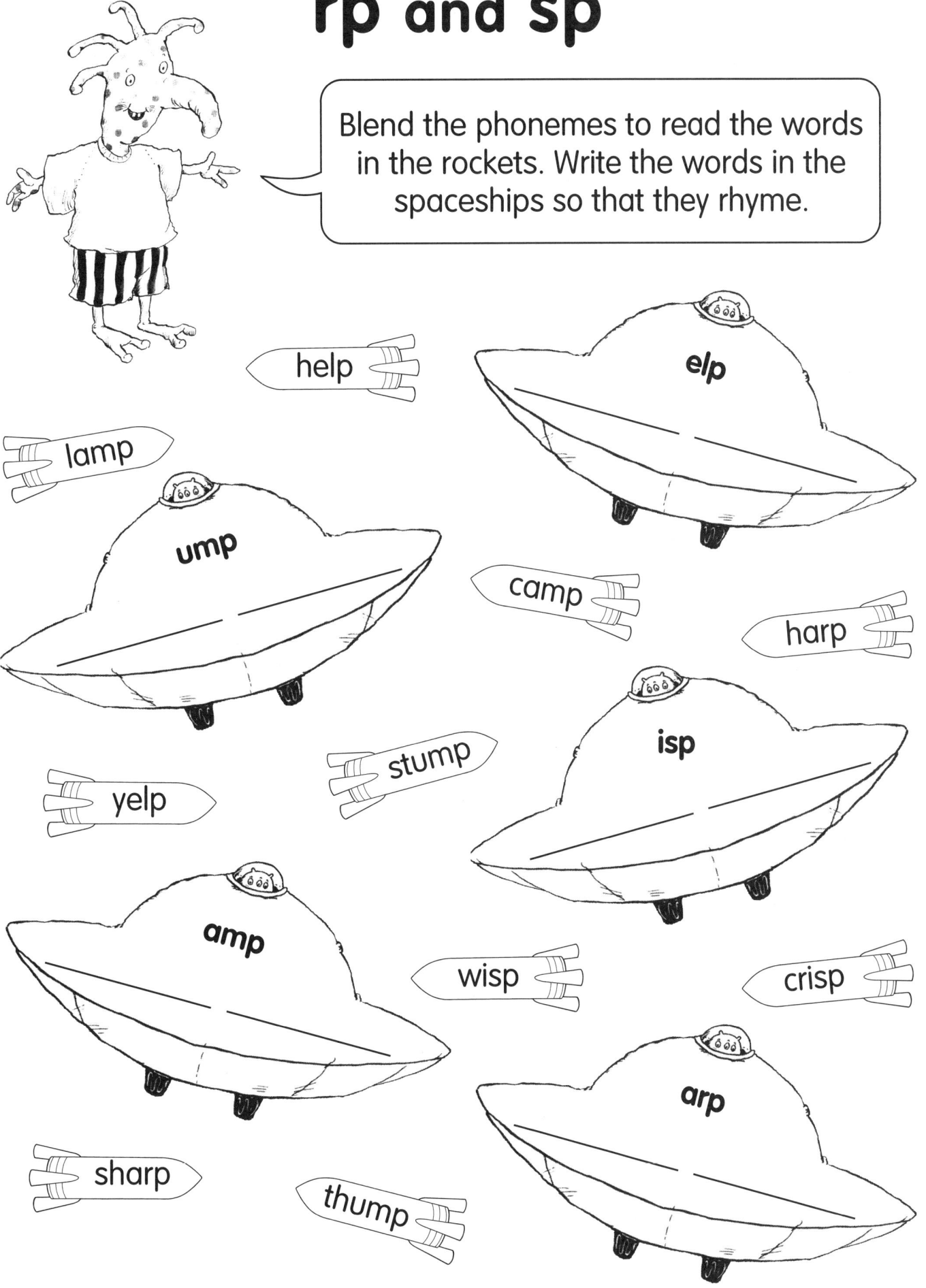

help

elp

lamp

ump

camp

harp

stump

isp

yelp

amp

wisp

crisp

arp

sharp

thump

Words that end in ct, ft, lt, nt, rt and st

Read the words in the rockets. Can you hear the blends at the end of the words? Join the pairs of words which have the same final blends. One pair has been joined for you.

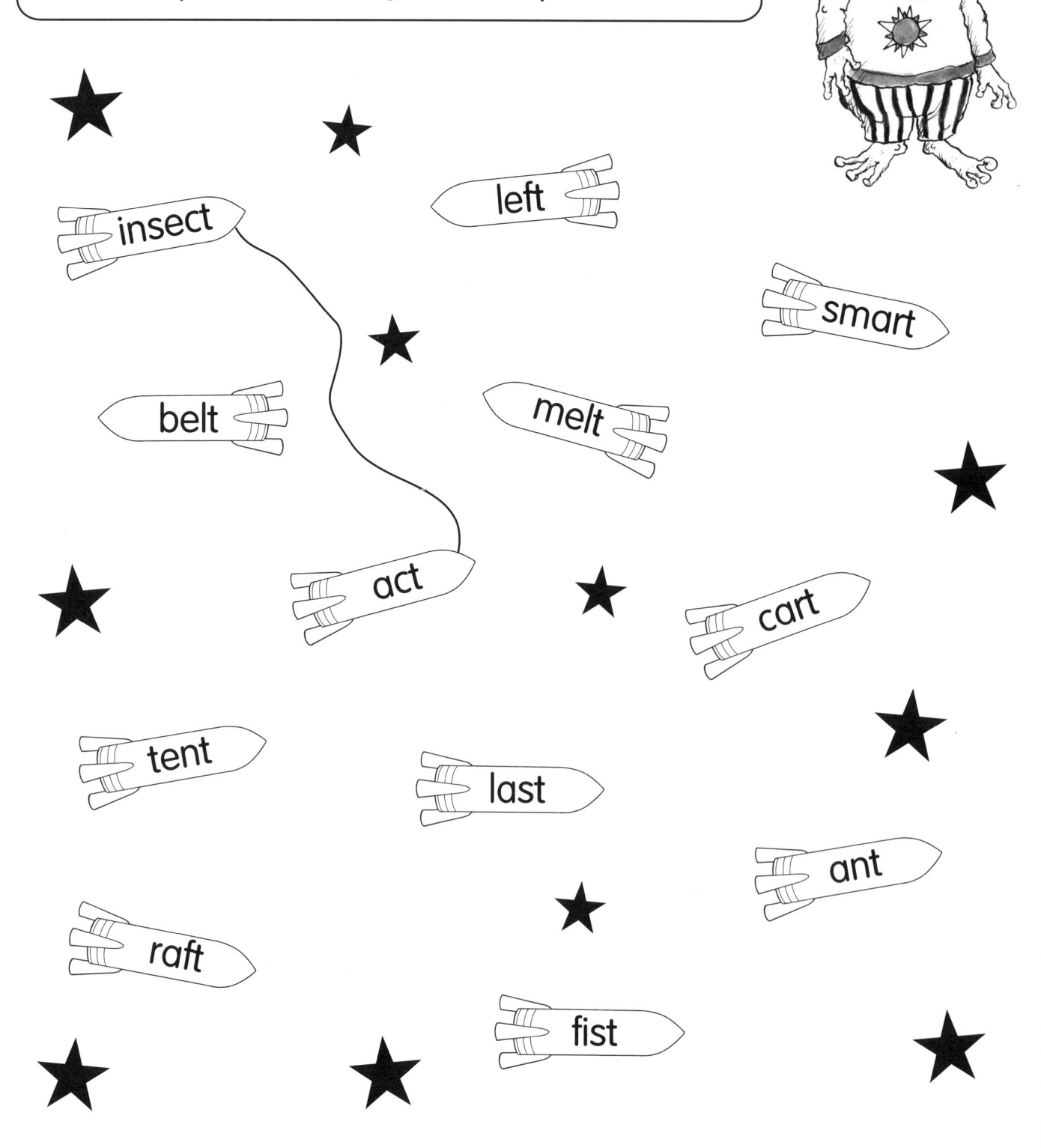

- insect
- left
- smart
- belt
- melt
- act
- cart
- tent
- last
- ant
- raft
- fist

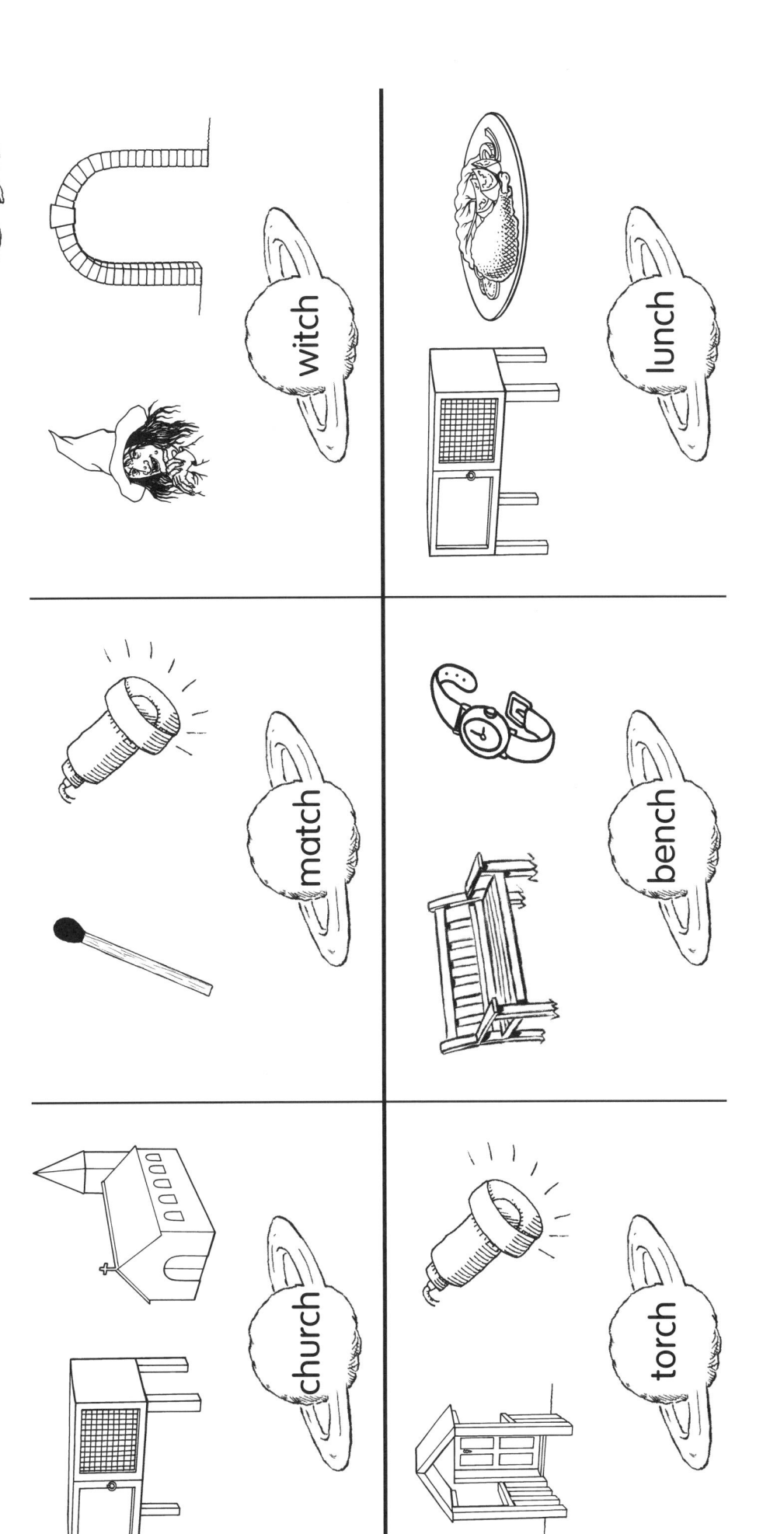

Words that end in nch, rch and tch

Look at the pictures and say what they show. Blend the phonemes to read the words in the planets. Can you hear the phonemes at the end of the word? Circle the correct picture for each word.

witch

lunch

match

bench

church

torch

Phonics and Spelling 2

Words that end in ff, ll, ss, ck and ng

Add the final phonemes to these letter strings and write the words on the lines. Use each ending twice. One has been done for you.

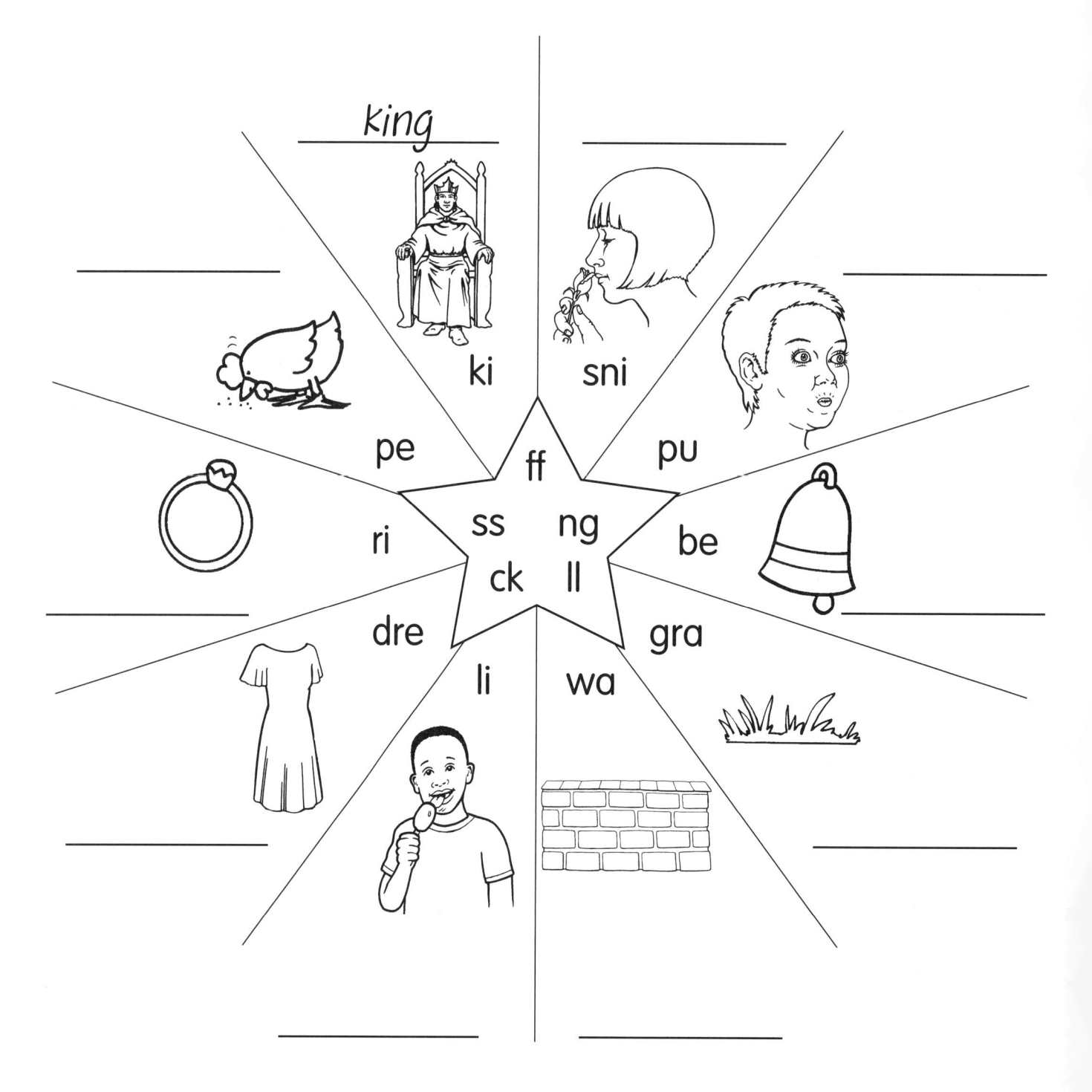

king

ki — sni — pu — be — gra — wa — li — dre — ri — pe

ff ss ng ck ll

Words that end in ck

Blend the phonemes to read the words in the word bank. Can you hear **ck** at the end of the words? Write the words in the pictures so that they rhyme.

Word bank

black check pack suck quick pick block
rock duck shock lick snack deck neck luck

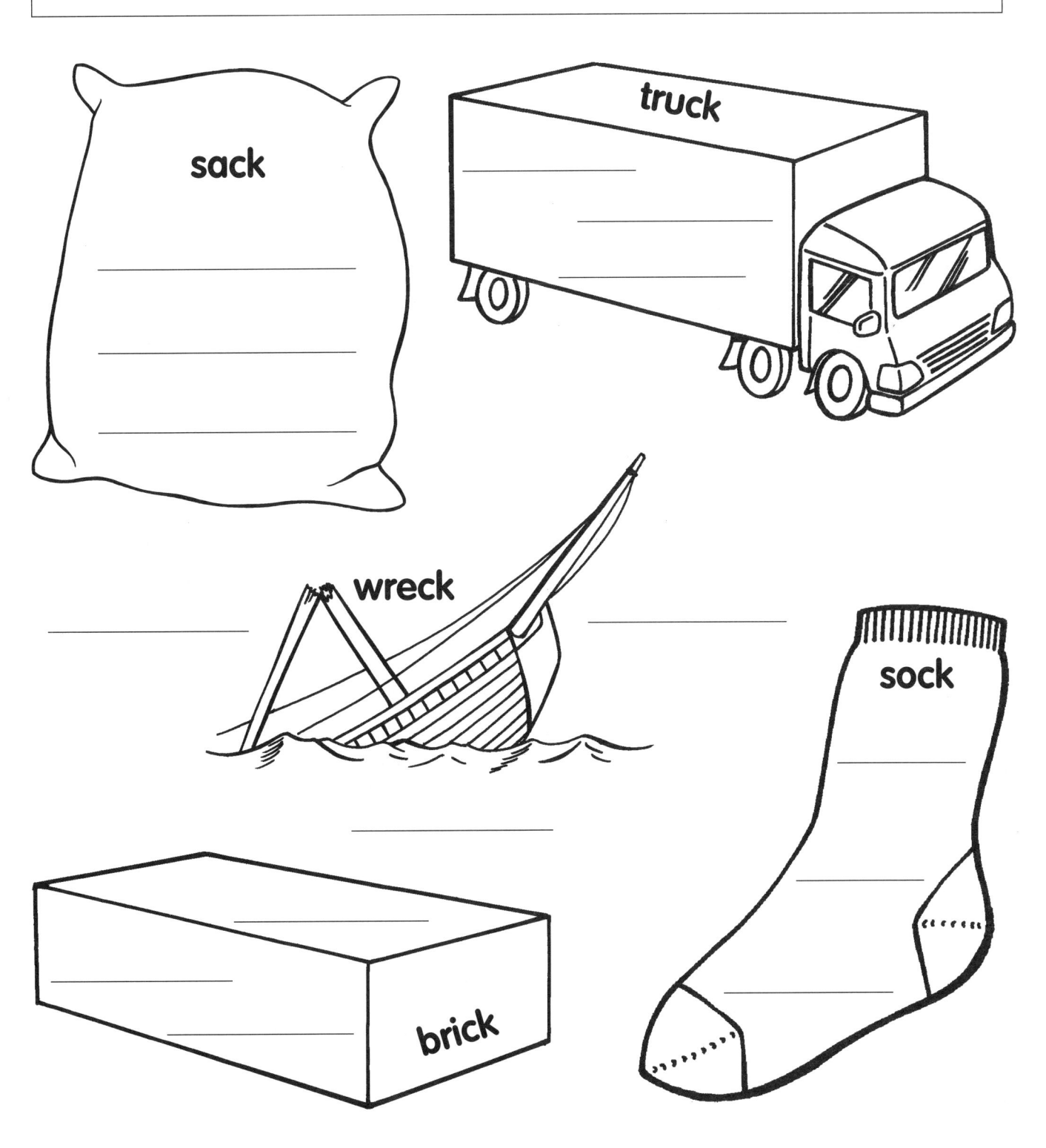

sack

truck

wreck

brick

sock

Words that end in ng

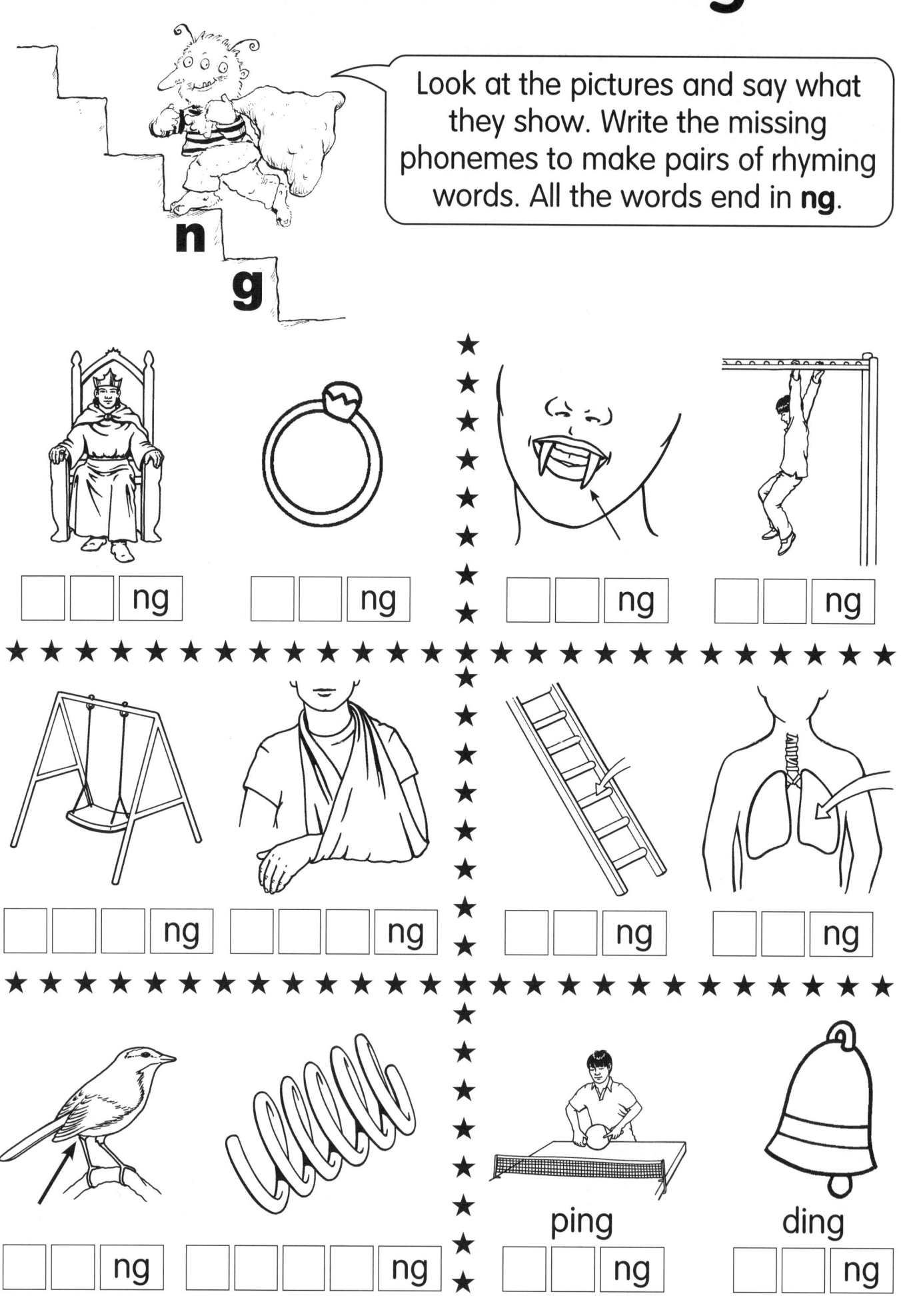

Look at the pictures and say what they show. Write the missing phonemes to make pairs of rhyming words. All the words end in **ng**.

☐ ☐ ng   ☐ ☐ ng   ☐ ☐ ng   ☐ ☐ ng

☐ ☐ ng   ☐ ☐ ☐ ng   ☐ ☐ ng   ☐ ☐ ng

☐ ☐ ng   ☐ ☐ ☐ ng   ping ☐ ng   ding ☐ ng

46   Phonics and Spelling 2   © HarperCollinsPublishers Limited 2011

Hard and soft g

Blend the phonemes to read these words:

g	a	t	e

b	a	g

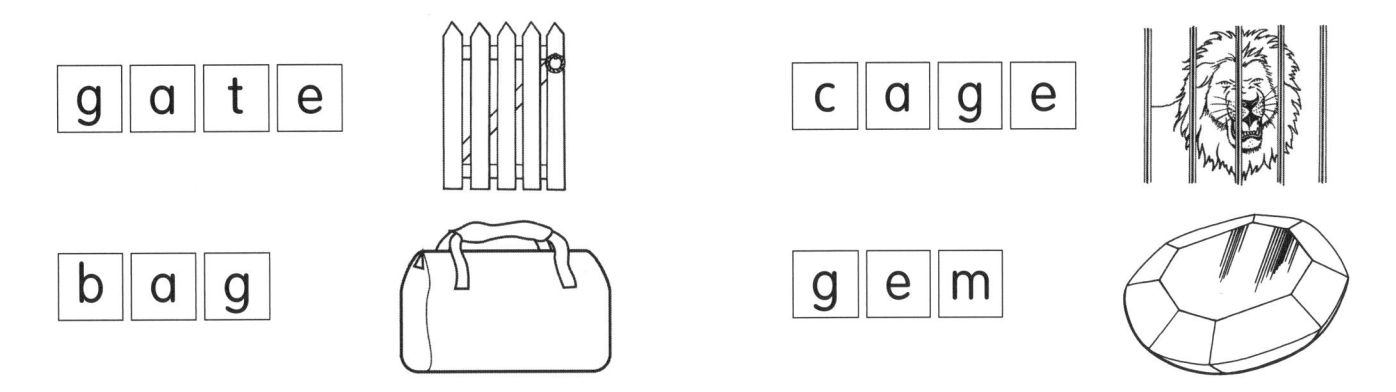

c	a	g	e

g	e	m

Can you hear the different **g** phonemes? The words *gate* and *bag* have a **hard g**. The words *cage* and *gem* have a **soft g**. This sounds like the phoneme **j**.

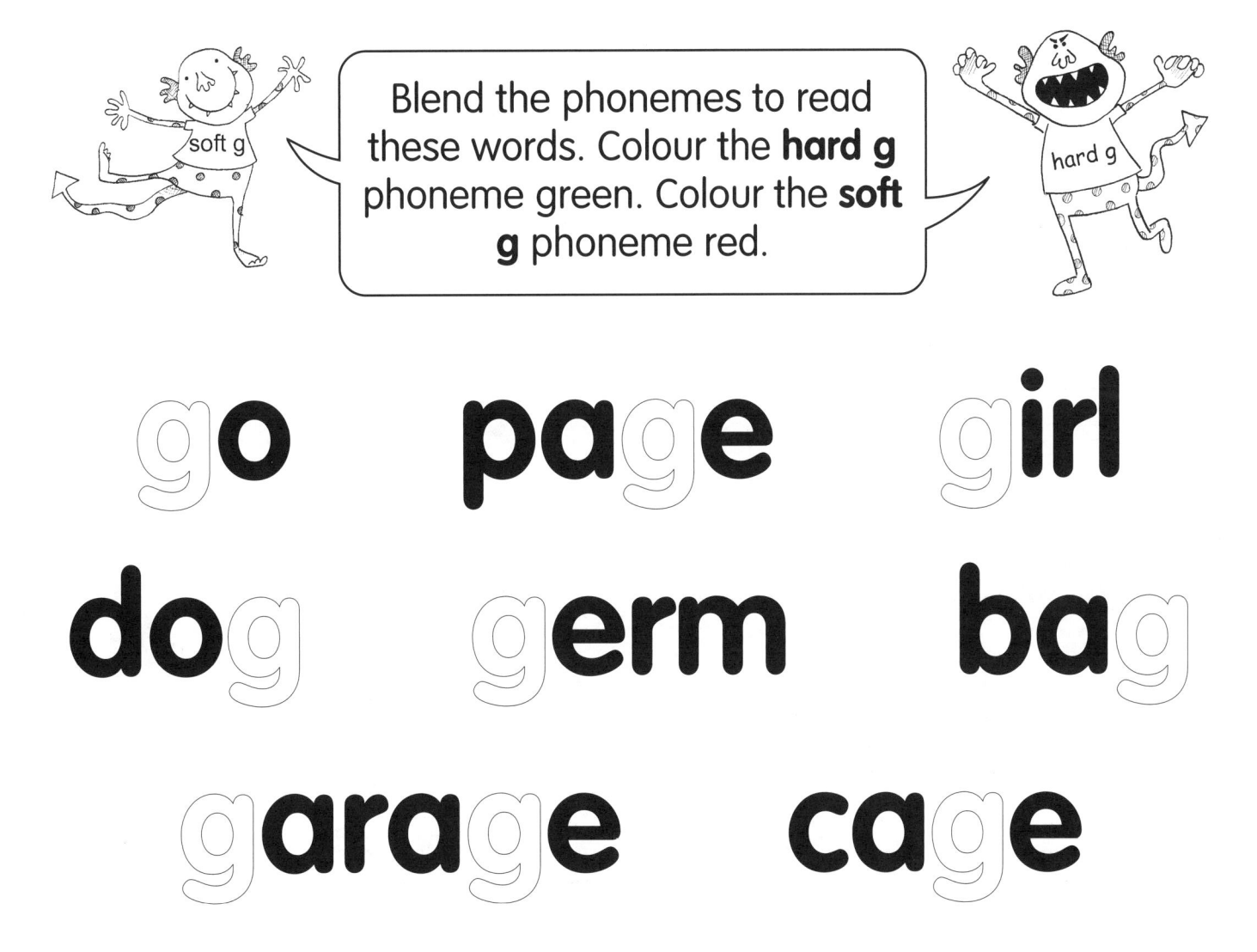

Blend the phonemes to read these words. Colour the **hard g** phoneme green. Colour the **soft g** phoneme red.

go   page   girl

dog   germ   bag

garage   cage

The ai phoneme spelt ay

The **ai** phoneme can be spelt **ay**, for example, *hay*, *say* and *may*.

Blend the phonemes to read the words in the word bank. Write them in this rocket puzzle. Some letters have been written in to help you. All the words end in **ay**.

Word bank

Friday   day   today
hay   say   away
play   lay   clay   way
Monday   pay

48   Phonics and Spelling 2   © HarperCollinsPublishers Limited 2011

The ai phoneme

Blend the phonemes to read these words: *make, day* and *rain*. They are not spelt the same, but can you hear that they all have the **ai** phoneme? This phoneme can be spelt **ai**, **ay** and **a-e**.

Look at these pictures and read the words. Circle the pictures with the **ai** phoneme. Remember, it can be spelt **ai**, **ay** or **a-e**.

safe   rat   rain   pram   pray

sail   cape   tray   spade   cap

★ ★ ★   ★ ★ ★   ★ ★ ★   ★ ★ ★

Phonics and Spelling 2

Words that rhyme using the ai phoneme

Look at the letters in the wings of the alien insects. They spell words that rhyme. Use them to write two rhyming words on the lines below. Remember, the **ai** phoneme can be spelt **ai**, **ay** or **a-e**.

_____

_____

_____

_____

_____

_____

_____

_____

The ee phoneme

Blend the phonemes to read these words: *he, see* and *leaf.* They are not spelt the same but can you hear that they all have the **ee** phoneme? This phoneme can be spelt **ee**, **ea** or **e**.

★★★ ★★★ ★★★ ★★★

Blend the phonemes to read these words. Colour the words with the **ee** phoneme. Remember, it can be spelt **ee**, **ea** or **e**. Be careful as some of the words are spelt with an **e** but do not have the **ee** phoneme.

bed   she   me

green   neck

sea   eat   bee

week   pet

Words that rhyme using the ee phoneme

Blend the phonemes to read the words at the bottom of the page. Look at the pictures and say what they show. Cut out the words and stick them around the picture that rhymes with the word. Words that rhyme are not always spelt in the same way.

tree

feet

bee	meat
seat	me
sea	sweet
tea	pea
three	treat
heat	see

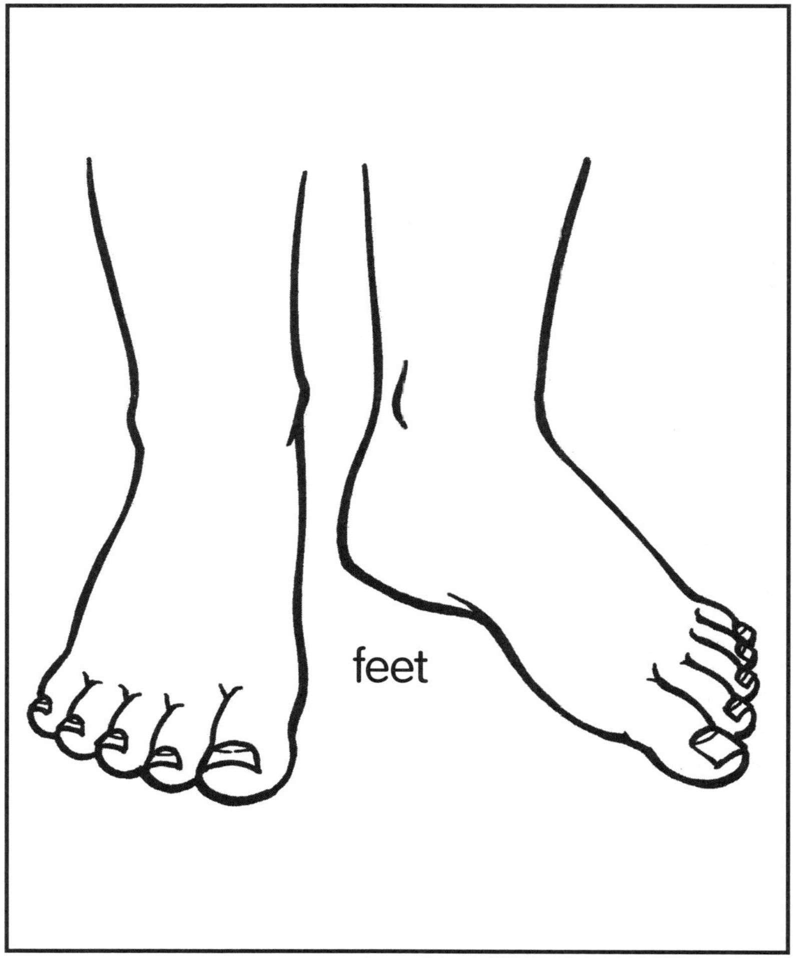

52   Phonics and Spelling 2   © HarperCollinsPublishers Limited 2011

The igh phoneme

Blend the phonemes to read these words: *try, pie, line* and *sigh*. They are not spelt the same but can you hear that they all have the **igh** phoneme? This phoneme can be spelt **igh**, **y**, **ie** and **i-e**.

Blend the phonemes to read these letter strings. Look at the pictures and say what they show. Cut out the letter strings and pictures. On a separate piece of paper, stick the letter strings together to make words with the **igh** phoneme. Stick the pictures next to the words.

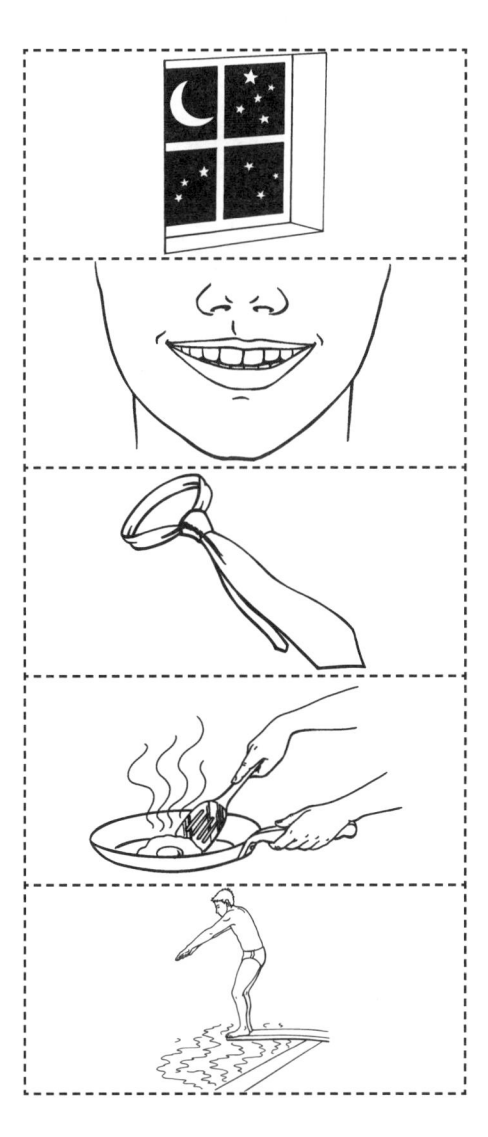

fr		ie
t		ight
n	+	ile
sm		y
d		ive

Phonics and Spelling 2

The igh phoneme

Blend the phonemes to read these words:

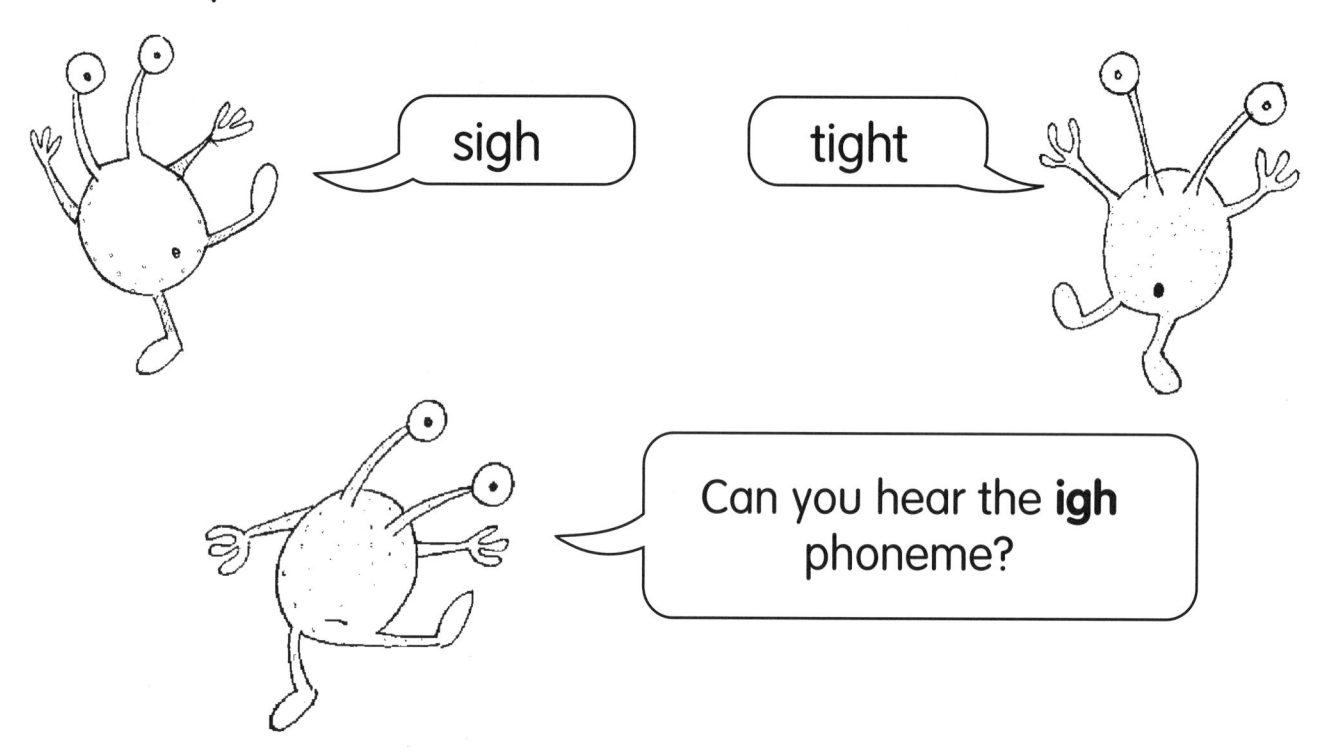

sigh

tight

Can you hear the **igh** phoneme?

Join these words to the pictures.

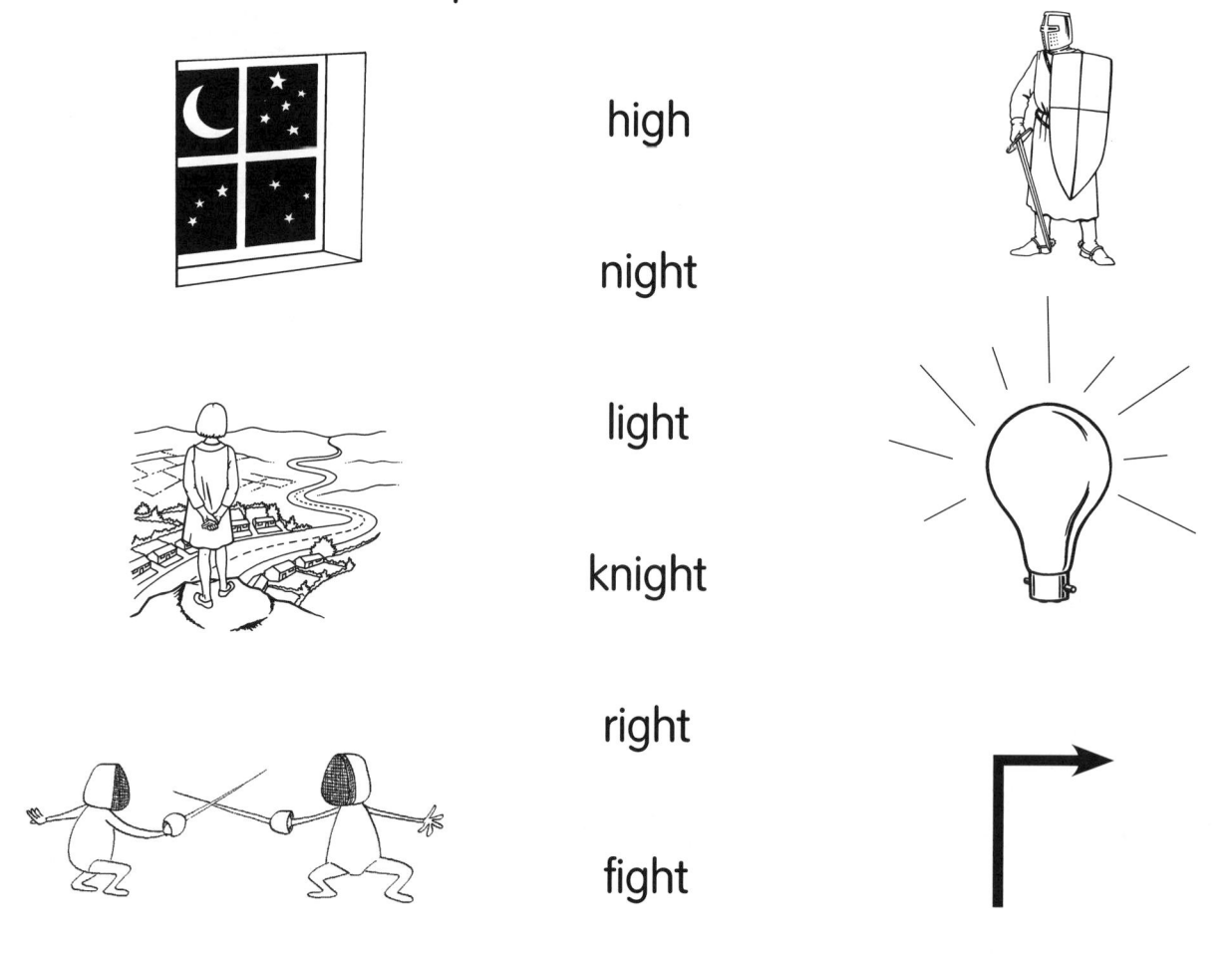

high

night

light

knight

right

fight

Words that rhyme using the igh phoneme

Read the word in the speech bubbles. In each letter puzzle there are four hidden words which rhyme with the word in the speech bubble. Circle the words. Words that rhyme do not have to be spelt in the same way.

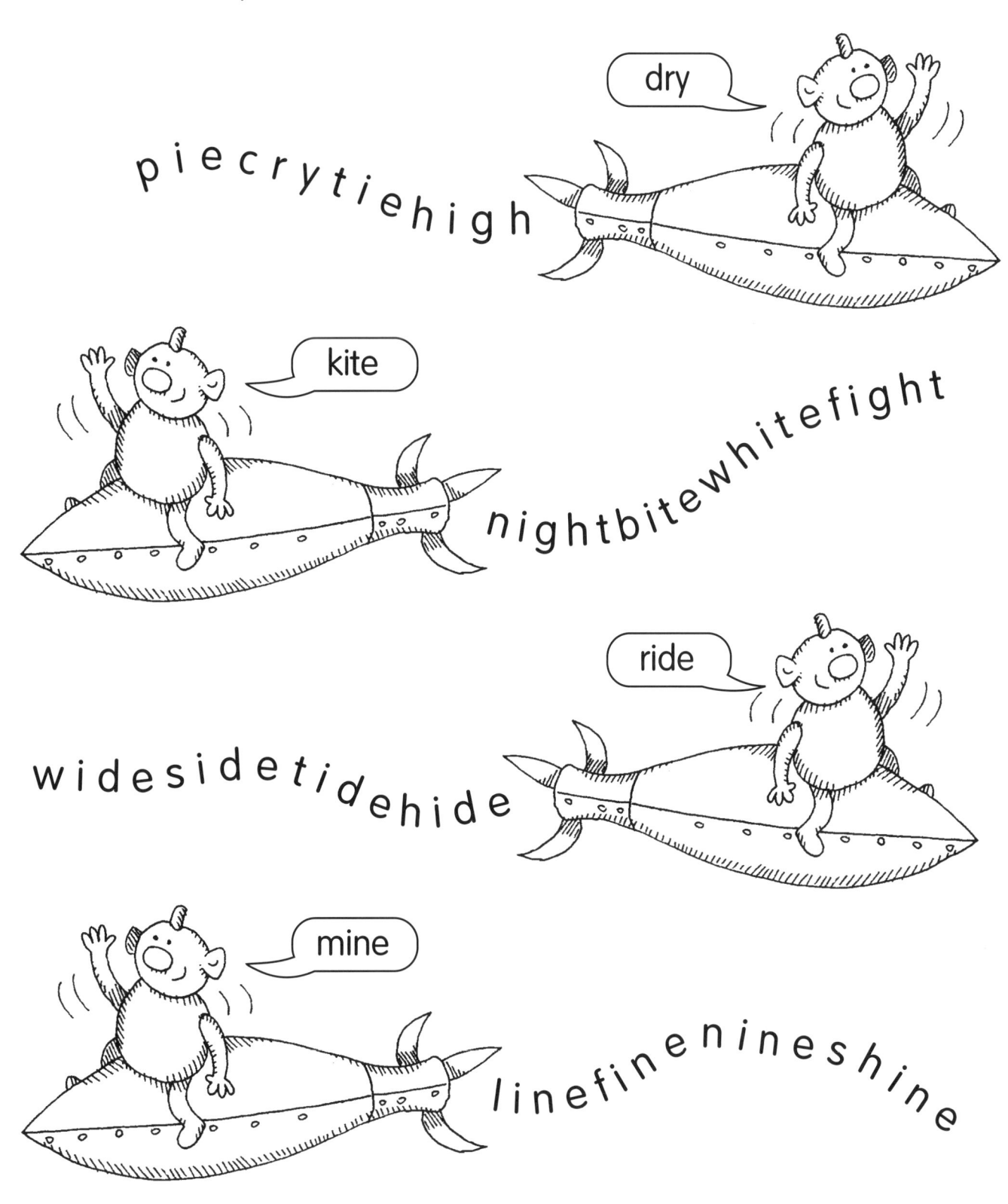

dry

piecrytiehigh

kite

nightbitewhitefight

ride

widesidetidehide

mine

linefinenineshine

The oa phoneme

Blend the phonemes to read these words: *no, low, home* and *foam*. They are not spelt the same but can you hear that they all have the **oa** phoneme? This phoneme can be spelt **oa, ow, o** or **o-e**.

Look at the pictures and say what they are. Use the phonemes to spell the words. Write them in the boxes.

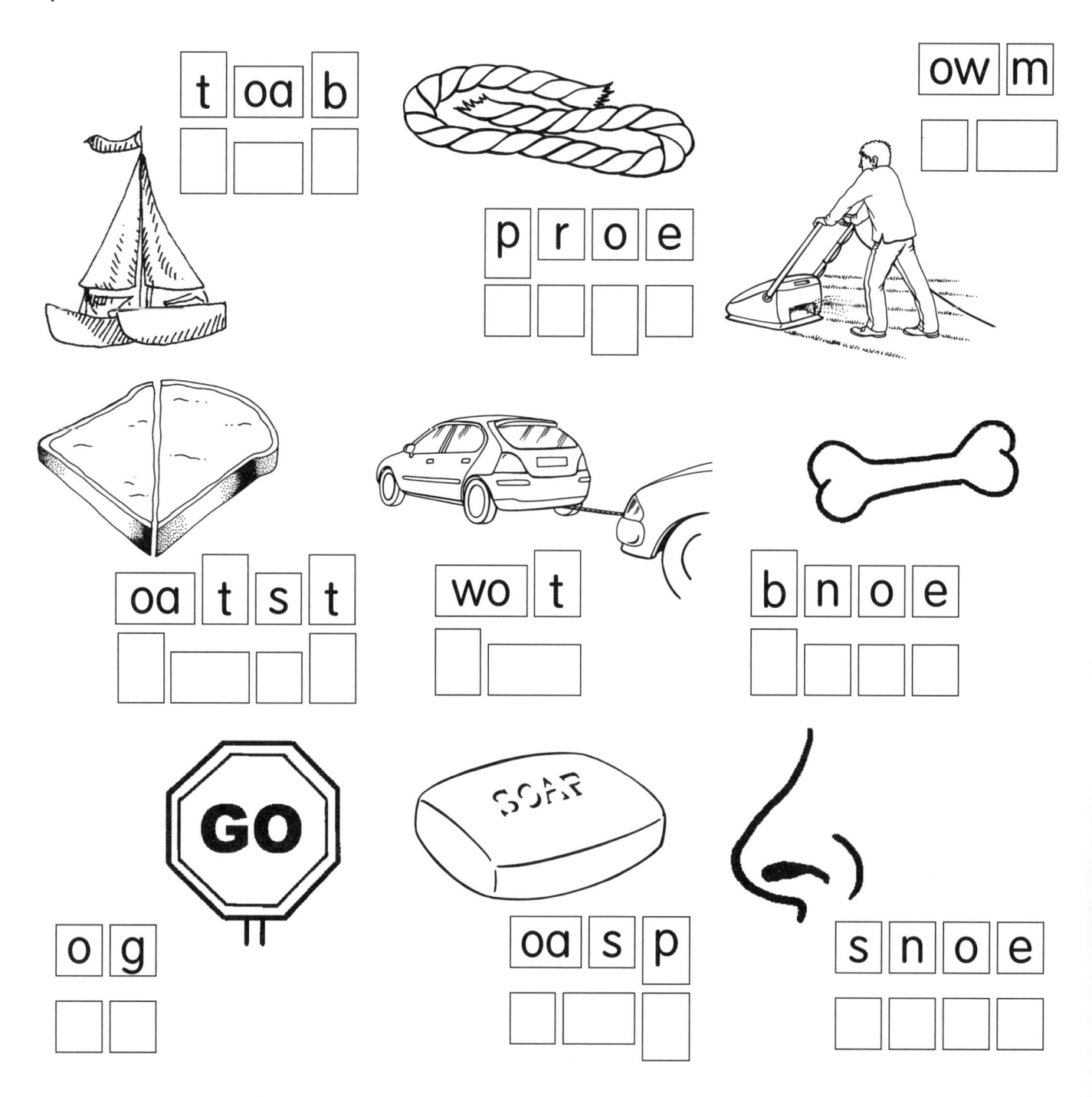

| t | oa | b |

| ow | m |

| p | r | o | e |

| oa | t | s | t |

| wo | t |

| b | n | o | e |

| o | g |

| oa | s | p |

| s | n | o | e |

56   Phonics and Spelling 2   © HarperCollinsPublishers Limited 2011

Words that rhyme using the oa phoneme

Look at the pictures. Blend the phonemes and say the words. Can you hear some words that rhyme? Write the words in the boxes in groups that rhyme.

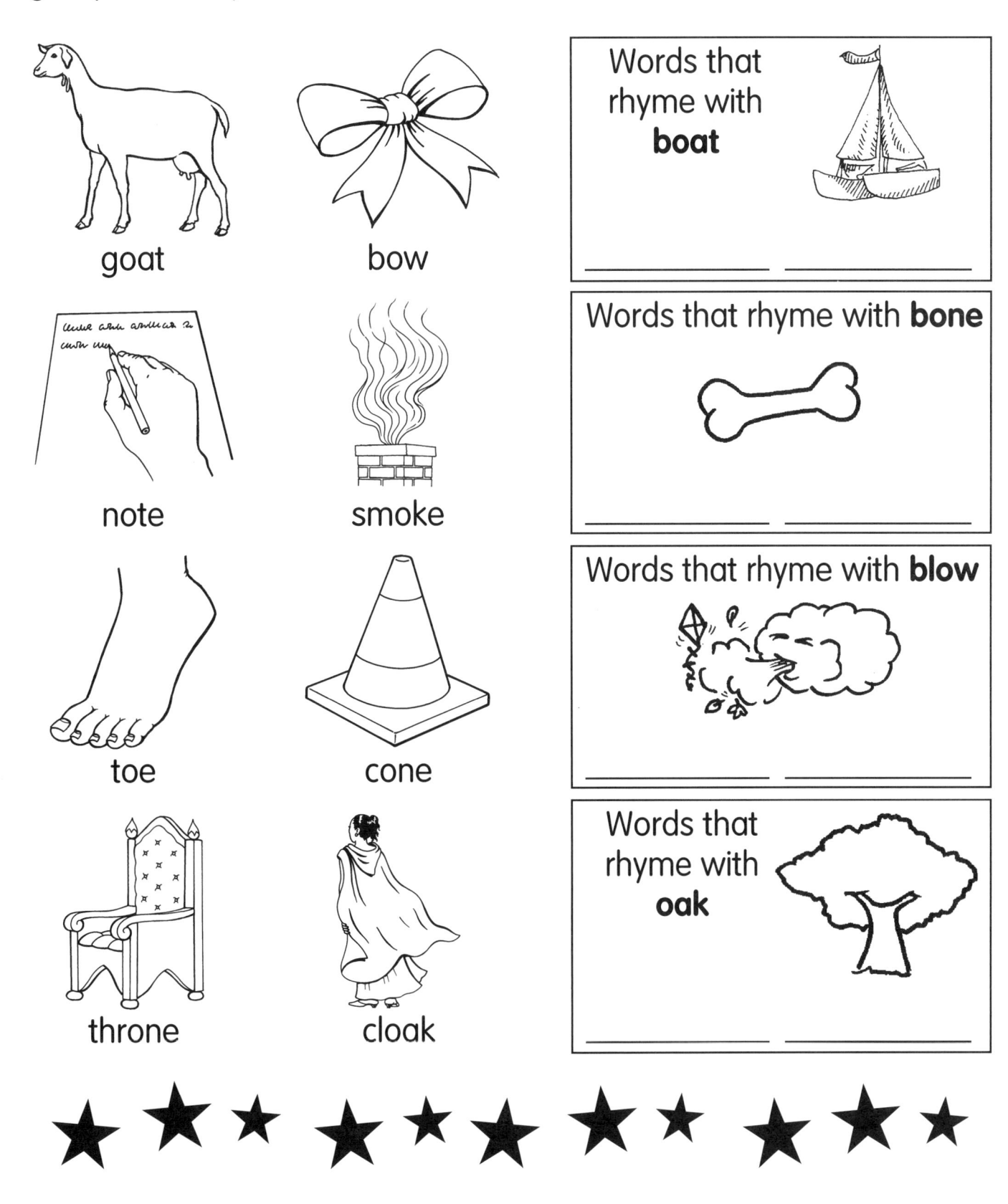

goat

bow

note

smoke

toe

cone

throne

cloak

Words that rhyme with **boat**
_____ _____

Words that rhyme with **bone**
_____ _____

Words that rhyme with **blow**
_____ _____

Words that rhyme with **oak**
_____ _____

Phonics and Spelling 2

The long oo phoneme

Blend the phonemes to read these words: *shoot, rule, blew* and *blue*. They are not spelt the same but can you hear that they have the same long **oo** phoneme? This can be spelt **oo**, **o-e**, **ew** or **ue**.

Join these phonemes together and write the words on the line. Then join them to the pictures.

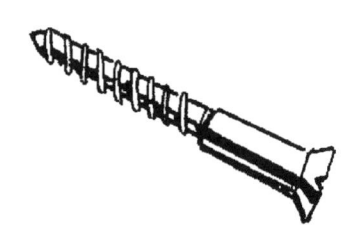

s + c + r + ew

= _____

m + oo + n

= _____

g + l + ue

= _____

sh + a + m + p + oo

= _____

Words that rhyme using the long OO phoneme

Blend the phonemes to read the words. Can you hear some words that rhyme? Join the rhyming words together. Remember, the rhyming words may not be spelt in the same way.

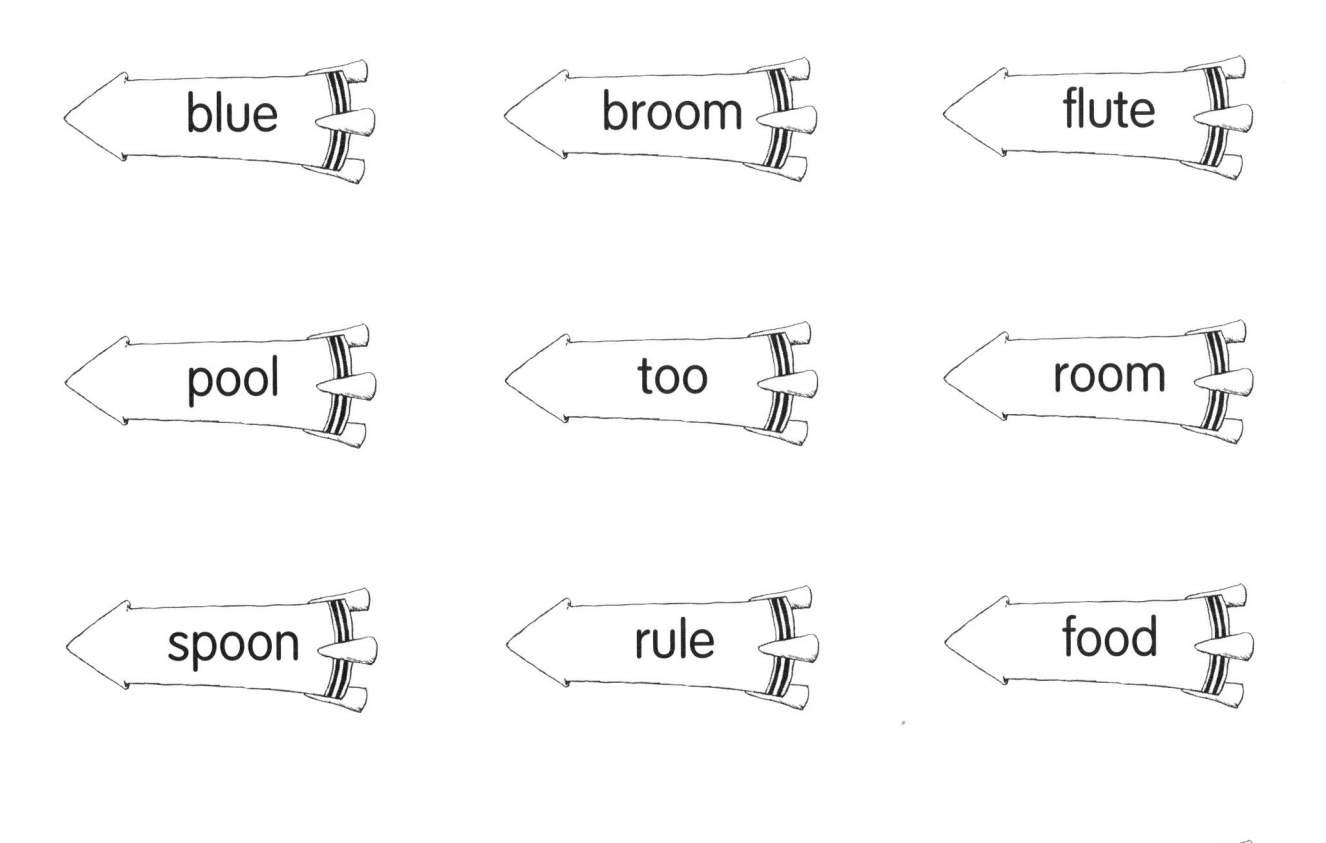

blue   broom   flute

pool   too   room

spoon   rule   food

rude   moon   boot

Words with ar

Look at the pictures and say what they show. All these words have the phoneme **ar**. Choose the correct phonemes to complete the words. Write the words on the lines. Blend the phonemes to read the words.

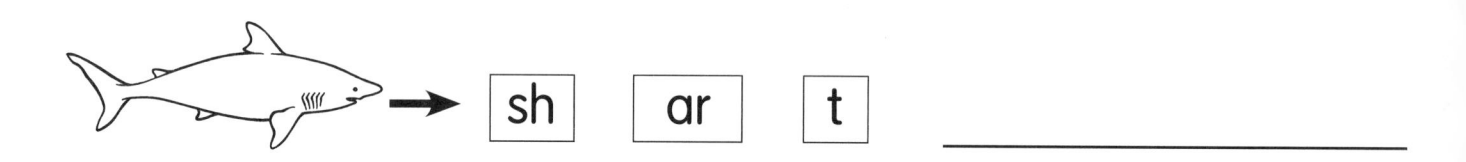

sh	ar	t	_____
d	ar	k	_____
f	ar	d	_____
c	ar	n	_____
b	ar	m	_____

Words with aw

Blend the phonemes to read this word: *saw*. Can you hear the **aw** sound?

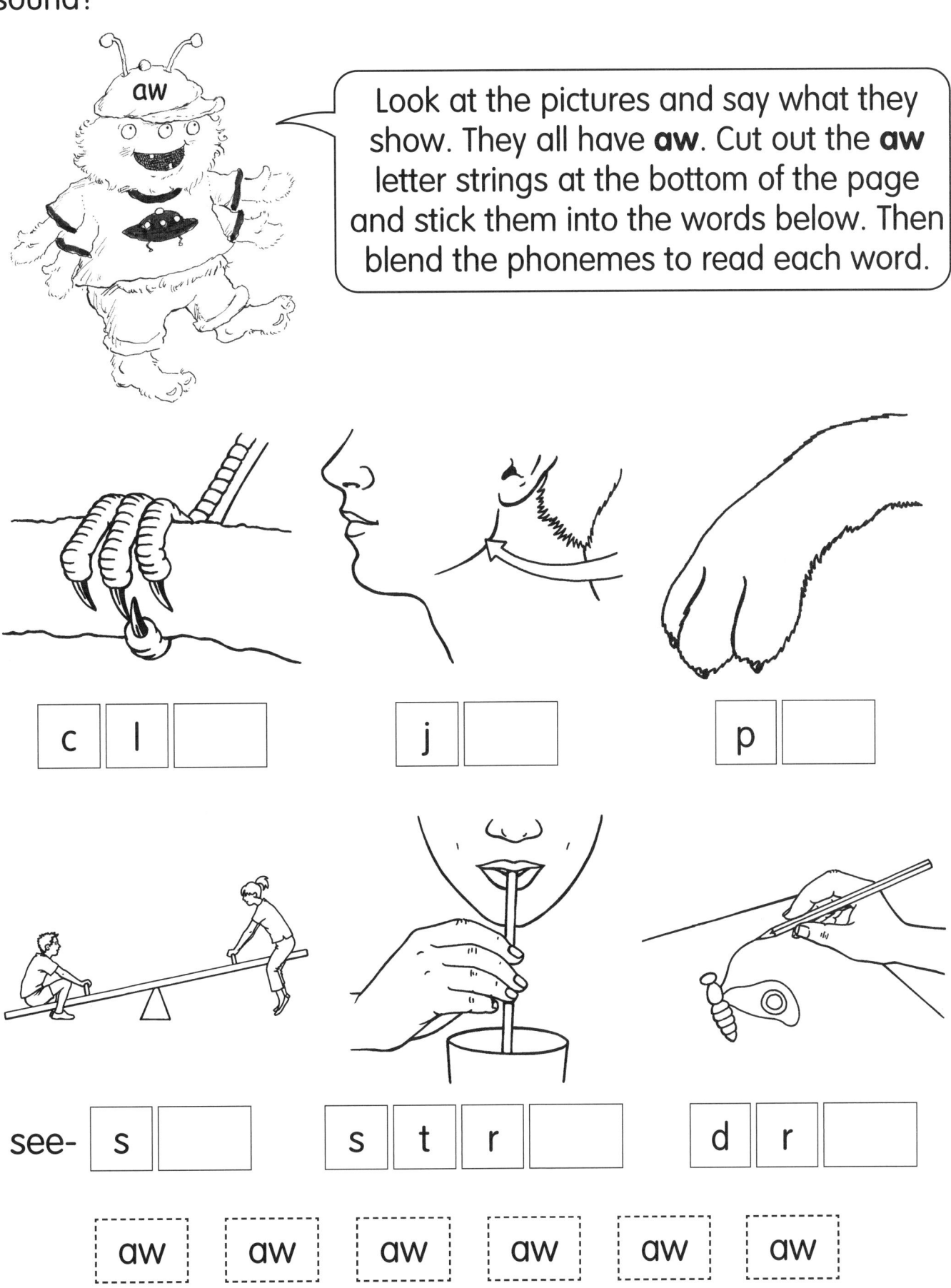

Look at the pictures and say what they show. They all have **aw**. Cut out the **aw** letter strings at the bottom of the page and stick them into the words below. Then blend the phonemes to read each word.

| c | l | | | j | | | p | |

see- | s | | | s | t | r | | | d | r |

| aw | | aw | | aw | | aw | | aw | | aw |

Phonics and Spelling 2

The Ur phoneme

Blend the phonemes and say these words: *her, girl* and *fur*. Can you hear the **ur** phoneme? It can be spelt **ur**, **er** or **ir**.

Choose the correct spelling of the phonemes for these words. Write the words on the lines. Blend the phonemes to read the words.

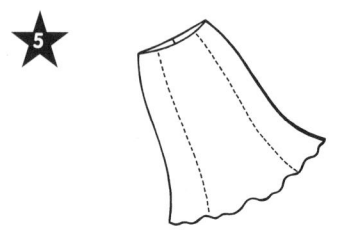

★1 b + er/ir/ur + d = _____

★2 s + er/ir/ur + f = _____

★3 f + er/ir/ur + n = _____

★4 b + er/ir/ur + n = _____

★5 sk + er/ir/ur + t = _____

Words with ea

Blend the phonemes to read these words: *sea* and *neat*. Can you hear the **ee** phoneme? This phoneme can be spelt **ea**.

Look at the pictures. Blend the phonemes to read the words. Colour the pictures with the **ee** phoneme spelt **ea**.

beads

meat

ice cream

bed

leaf

beak

beach

shed

peg

Phonics and Spelling 2

63

Words with air, are, ear and ere

Blend the phonemes to read these words:

| h | air |

| c | are |

| b | ear |

| th | ere |

Can you hear the **air** phoneme in these words? Can you see the different spellings? Look at the pictures and cut them out. Blend the phonemes to read the words at the bottom of the page and cut them out. Match the pictures to the words and stick them on a separate piece of paper.

| scare | pear | hare | chair | pair | where | bear | fair |

Phonics and Spelling 2 © HarperCollinsPublishers Limited 2011

Words with ow

Blend the phonemes to read these words:

| t | ow | n | | s | l | ow |

Can you hear the difference?

Look at the pictures. Blend the phonemes to read the words. Colour those which rhyme with the **ow** phoneme in *town*. Circle those which rhyme with the **ow** phoneme in *slow*.

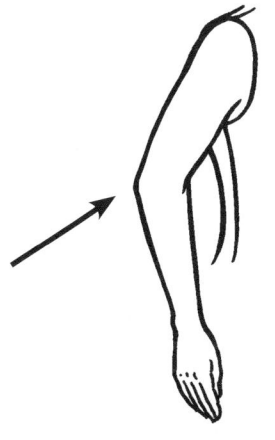

row

bow

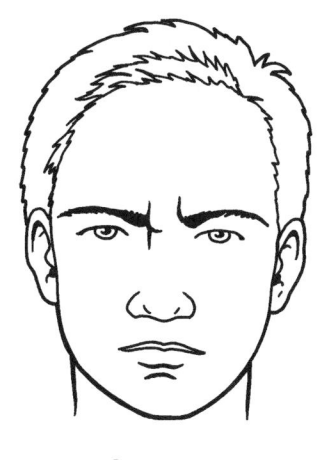

elbow

frown

crown

snow

Words with oo

Blend the phonemes to read these words: *good* and *room*. Can you hear the difference? Look at these pictures and read the words. Write words with a long **oo** phoneme in the pool and words with a short **oo** phoneme in the book.

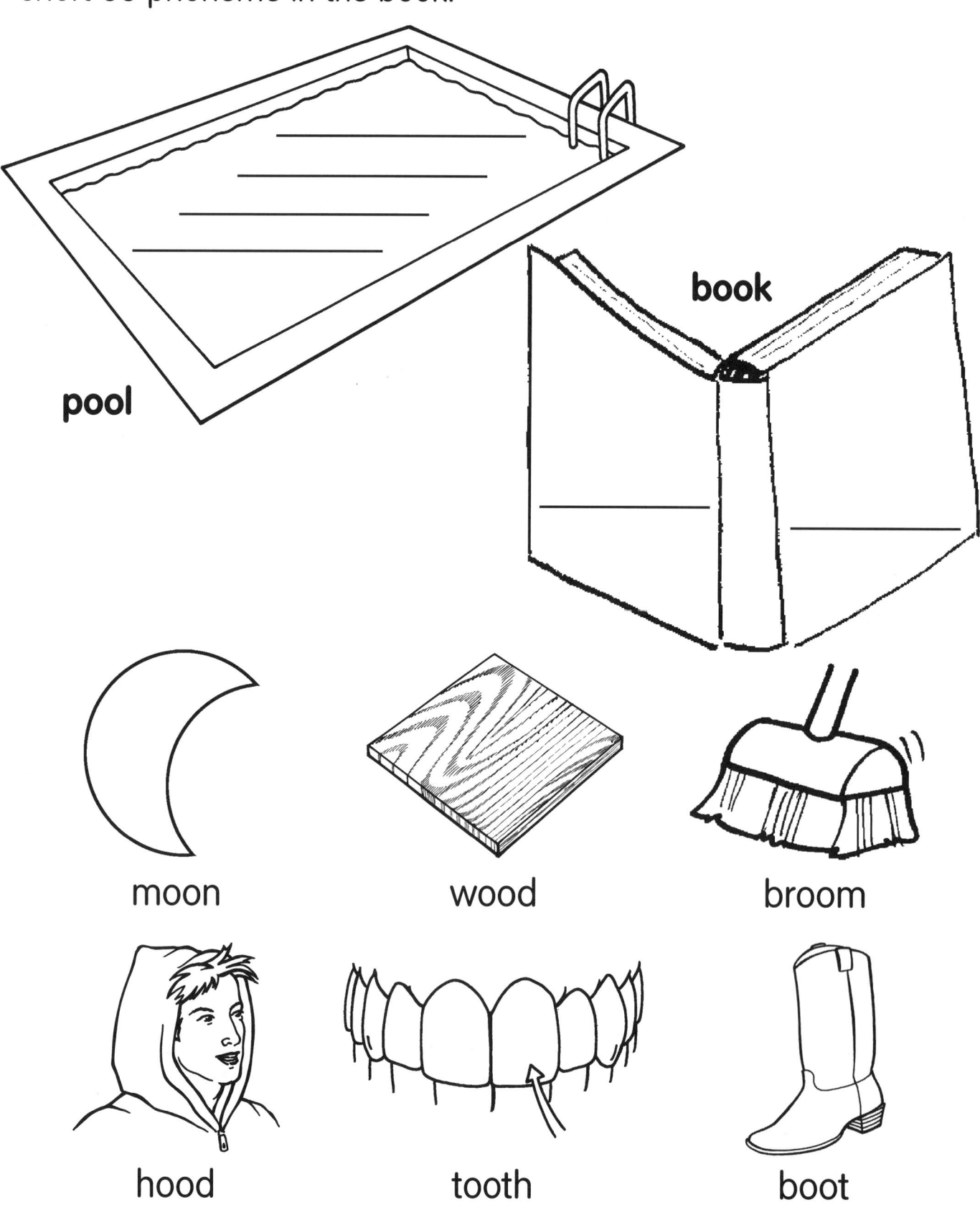

pool

book

moon

wood

broom

hood

tooth

boot

The oi phoneme

Blend the phonemes to read these words: *boy* and *coil*. The phoneme **oi** can be spelt **oy**.

★★★ ★★★ ★★★ ★★★

Blend the phonemes to read these words. Colour **oy** red. Colour **oi** blue.

toilet

toy

coin

soil

boy

The Or phoneme

Blend the phonemes to read these words: *for, floor* and *more*. The phoneme **or** can be spelt **or**, **oor** and **ore**.

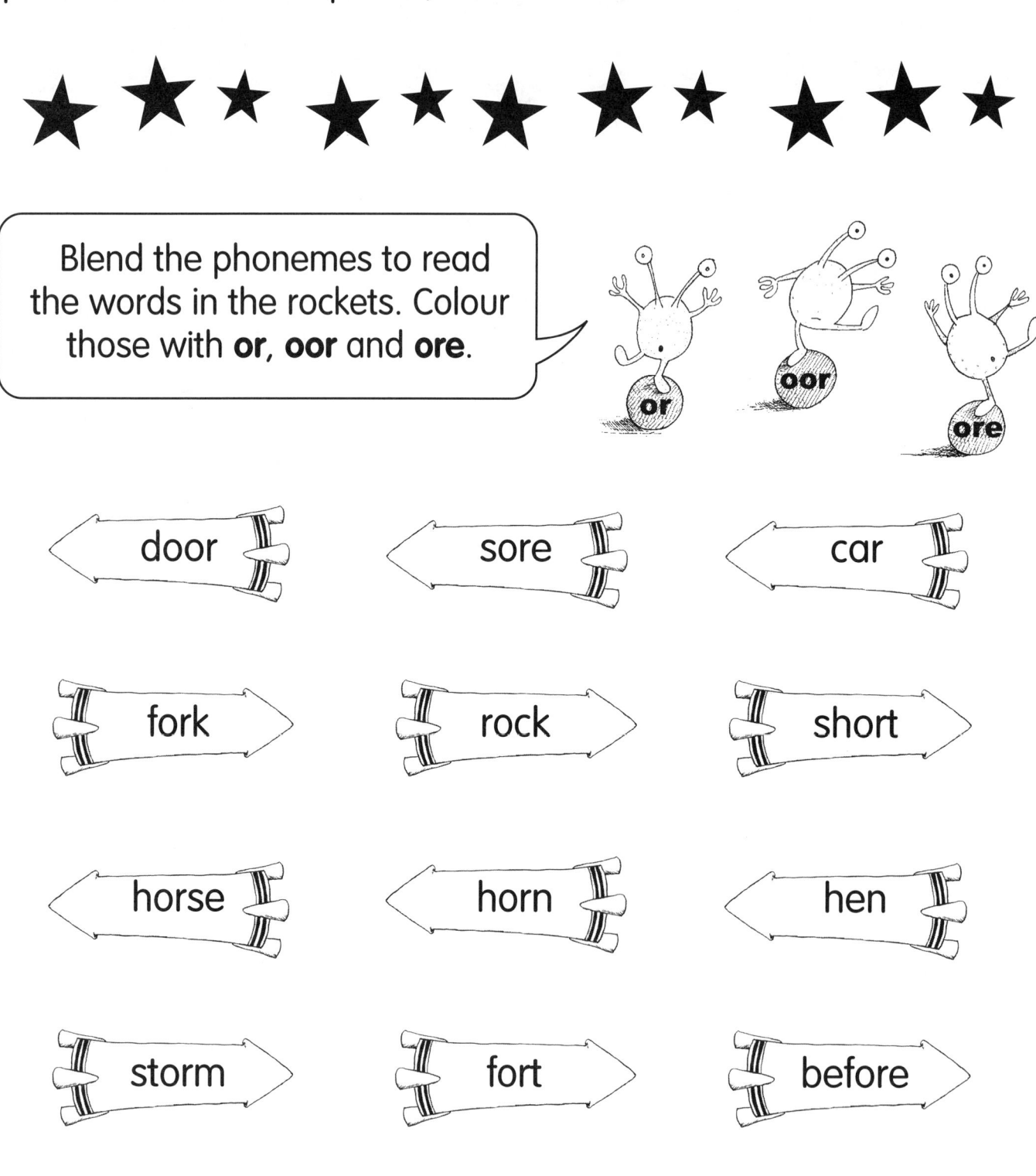

★ ★ ★ ★ ★ ★ ★ ★ ★ ★ ★

Blend the phonemes to read the words in the rockets. Colour those with **or**, **oor** and **ore**.

door — sore — car

fork — rock — short

horse — horn — hen

storm — fort — before

★ ★ ★ ★ ★ ★ ★ ★ ★ ★ ★

Plurals

Read the sentences. Change the words in the planets to plurals by adding **s**, for example, *brick – bricks*. Complete the sentences.

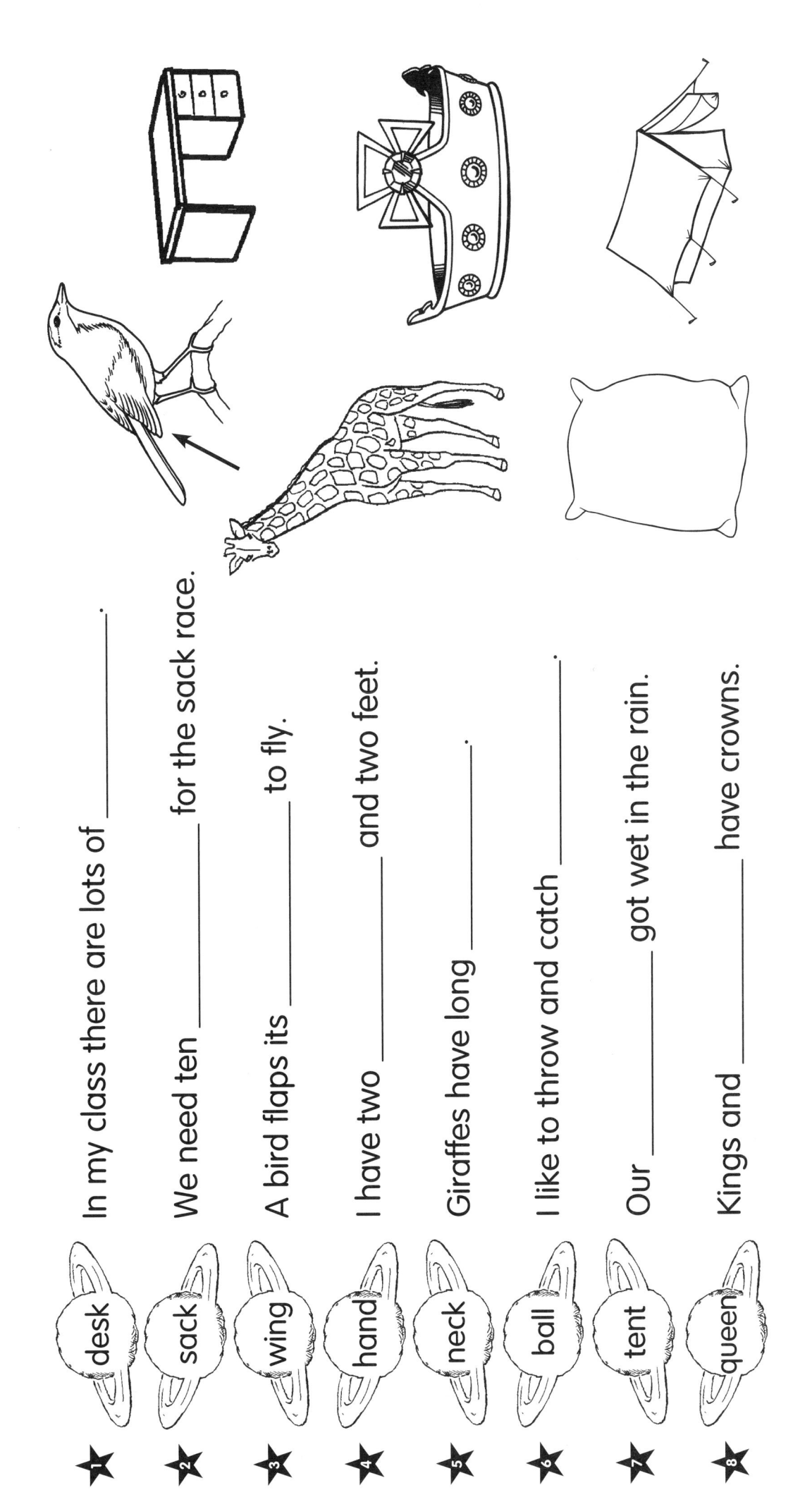

⭐1 desk   In my class there are lots of _____.

⭐2 sack   We need ten _____ for the sack race.

⭐3 wing   A bird flaps its _____ to fly.

⭐4 hand   I have two _____ and two feet.

⭐5 neck   Giraffes have long _____.

⭐6 ball   I like to throw and catch _____.

⭐7 tent   Our _____ got wet in the rain.

⭐8 queen   Kings and _____ have crowns.

Adding ed

Read this sentence: *Last week I bumped my head.* Can you see that the word *bump* has **ed** on the end?

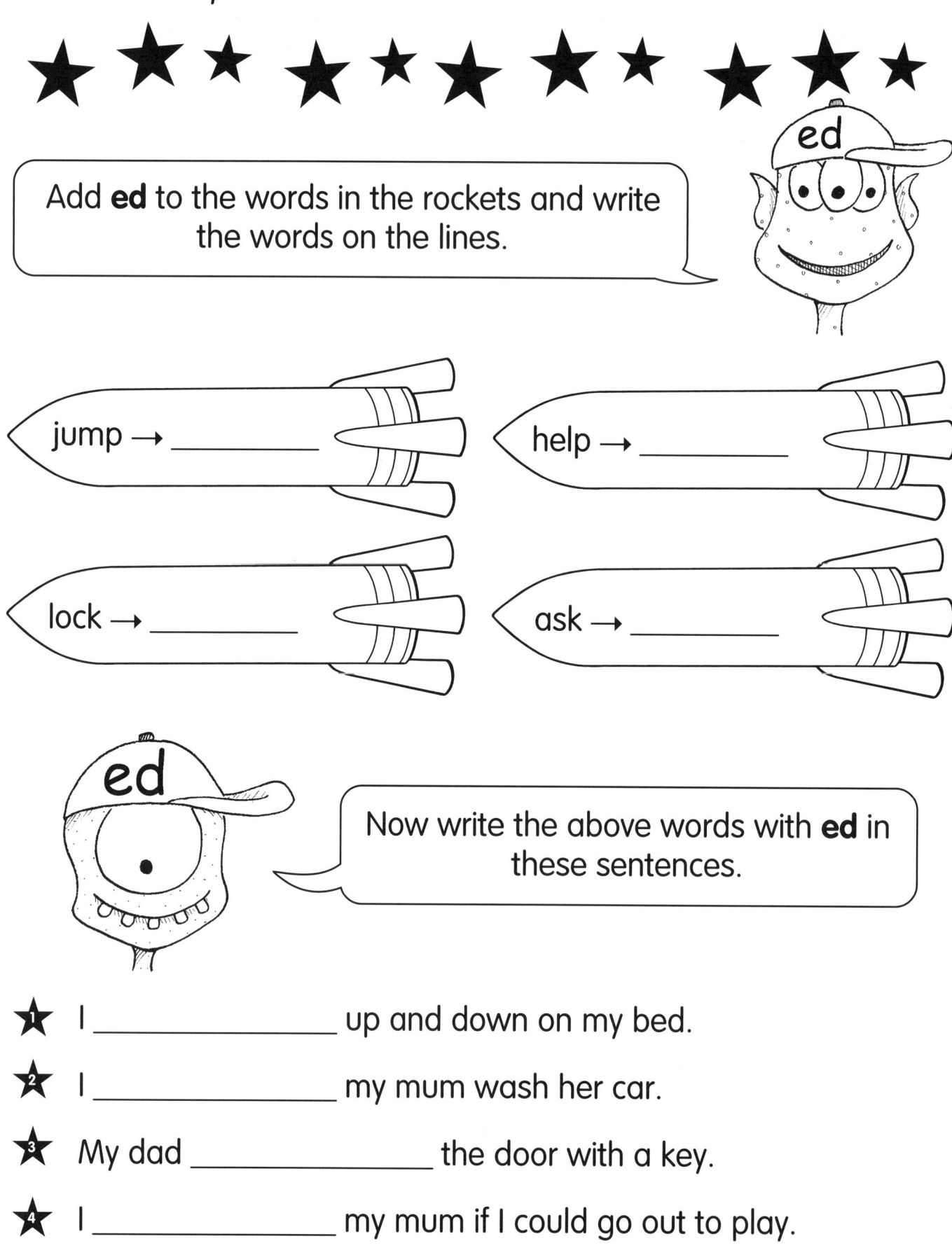

★ ★ ★ ★ ★ ★ ★ ★ ★ ★ ★ ★

Add **ed** to the words in the rockets and write the words on the lines.

jump → _____

help → _____

lock → _____

ask → _____

Now write the above words with **ed** in these sentences.

★1 I _____ up and down on my bed.

★2 I _____ my mum wash her car.

★3 My dad _____ the door with a key.

★4 I _____ my mum if I could go out to play.

Adding ing

Read this sentence: *I am going home soon.* Can you see that the word *go* has **ing** on the end?

Add **ing** to the words in the spaceships and write the words on the lines.

sink

kick

walk

jump

Phonics and Spelling 2

Words that end in y

Blend the phonemes to read these words: *hairy* and *teddy*. Can you hear the phoneme **ee** at the end? This phoneme can be spelt with a **y**.

Blend the phonemes to read the words in the spaceship. Join each word to a picture.

fairy   puppy
baby   cherry   teddy
dirty

Phonics and Spelling 2

Words with double letters

Blend the phonemes to read these words: *letter*, *correct* and *running*. They have two letters in the middle which are the same.

Look at the pictures and say what they show. Write the double letters from the box below in the middle of each word. The last word has no picture clue to help you!

| tt | pp | mm | nn | ff | bb |

1. ho __ __ ing
2. bu __ __ on
3. to __ __ ee
4. ke __ __ el
5. ro __ __ er
6. su __ __ er

Phonics and Spelling 2

Words with er

Blend the phonemes to read these words: *louder, sweeter, teacher* and *singer*. Can you hear **er** at the end of each word?

Blend the phonemes to read the words in the rockets. Break them up as in the example.

Example: jumper = jump + er

duster = ___ + ___

quicker = ___ + ___

cracker = ___ + ___

older = ___ + ___

taller = ___ + ___

walker = ___ + ___

recorder = ___ + ___

Words with ly

Blend the phonemes to read these words: *sweetly* and *loudly*. Can you hear **ly** at the end of each word?

Read the letters and letter strings below. Choose a letter or letter string from each rocket to spell words that end in **ly**. Write them on the lines. One has been done as an example.

Rocket 1: n, s, qu, n, b, gl, n, s

Rocket 2: ick, ad, ice, ad, eat, um, oft, ear

+ ly

nicely

Syllables

Blend the phonemes to read these words: *rib, ribbon* and *robbery*. Can you hear how many syllables each word has?

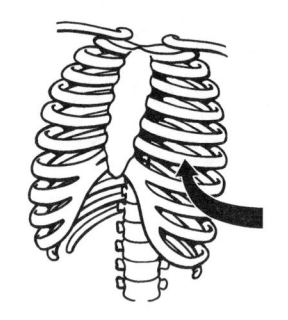

rib = 1 syllable   ribbon = 2 syllables   robbery = 3 syllables

Write your first name on the line. _____

How many syllables does your first name have? _____

Write your last name on the line. _____

How many syllables does your last name have? _____

Write the number of syllables of the words below in the stars.

this   =   ☆   Saturday = ☆   yellow = ☆

mother   =   ☆   name   = ☆   garden = ☆

door   =   ☆   suddenly = ☆   light   = ☆

morning   =   ☆   window   = ☆   ball   = ☆

Compound words

Blend the phonemes to read these words:

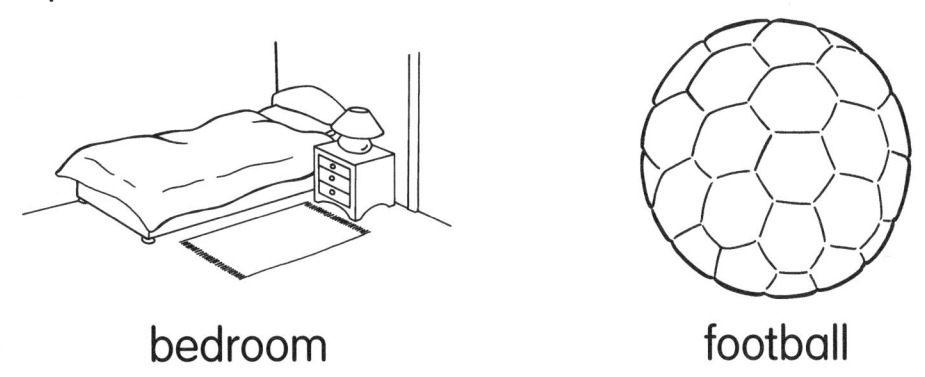

bedroom   football

Can you hear the two small words that make the big word?

Blend the phonemes to read the small words in the table below. Join them together to write a big word. Cut out the pictures and stick them next to the words.

Small words	Big word	Picture
cow + boy		
ear + ring		
toe + nail		
jelly + fish		
scare + crow		

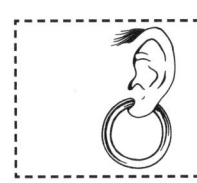

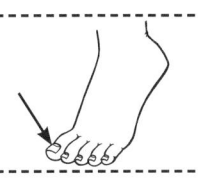

Phonics and Spelling 2

Things at school (nouns)

Blend the phonemes to read the words. Look at the picture. Cut out the words and stick them on the picture in the correct places.

pen	chair
door	book
girl	ball
desk	table
window	light
boy	bat

78   Phonics and Spelling 2   © HarperCollinsPublishers Limited 2011

Things in the garden (nouns)

Blend the phonemes to read the words. Look at the picture. Cut out the words and stick them on the picture in the correct places.

gate	dog
roof	peg
pond	bin
flower	cat
tree	slug
path	snail
grass	sun

© HarperCollinsPublishers Limited 2011   Phonics and Spelling 2   79

Opposites (antonyms)

> Blend the phonemes to read these words: *hot – cold*. These words have opposite meanings and are called **antonyms**. Blend the phonemes to read the words below. Cut out the words at the bottom of the page and stick them next to their opposites.

short

fast

fat

old

dry

sad

him

hard

first

small

| tall | thin | big | slow | her |
| happy | soft | wet | new | last |

Words with un and dis

Blend the phonemes to read these sentences:

I am happy, but he is unhappy.
I like jam but I dislike butter.

Can you see that the words *happy* and *like* have **un** and **dis** in front of them? The letter strings **un** and **dis** make the words mean the opposite. Add **un** and **dis** to these words and write them on the lines.

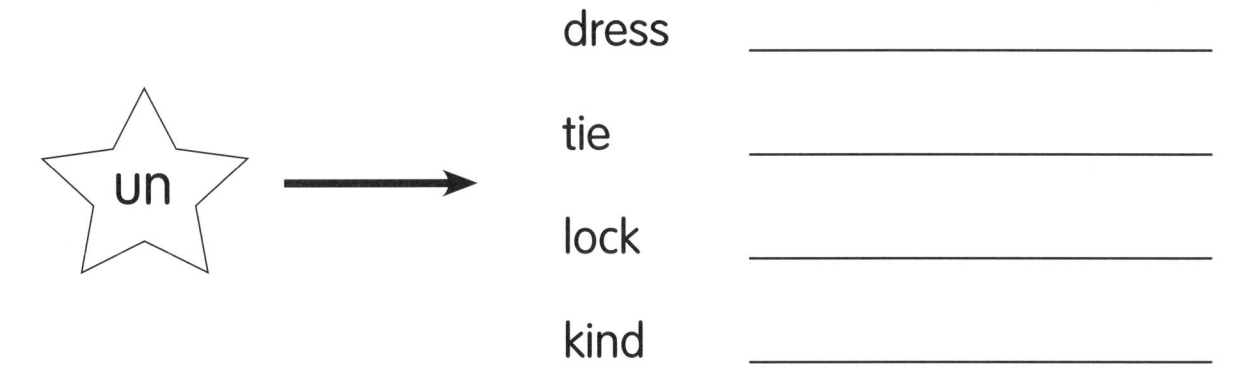

un ⟶

dress _____

tie _____

lock _____

kind _____

★★★★★★★★★★★★★★★★★★★★★★★★★★★★

dis ⟶

cover _____

agree _____

appear _____

Circle the correct words in these sentences.

★1 I **undress/unkind** when I have a bath.
★2 To take off my shoes I **unlock/untie** the laces.
★3 We **unhappy/unlock** the door to get in.
★4 The ugly sisters were **unkind/untie** to Cinderella.
★5 The aliens wanted to **disagree/discover** new planets.
★6 My sister and I always **disagree/disappear**.

High frequency words

Blend the phonemes to read the words in the walls. Write the words in the word grids. Look at the letters in the words carefully to see where they will fit. Some letters have been written in the grids to help you. Find the hidden word shaded in each grid and write it in on the line.

on | all | you | like

Hidden word: _____

was | yes | and | play

Hidden word: _____

she | the | see | going

Hidden word: _____

82   Phonics and Spelling 2   © HarperCollinsPublishers Limited 2011

High frequency words in sentences

Read the sentences. Write the missing words in the gaps. The words you need are in the rockets.

★1 My mum _____ I are _____ to the shops.   [going and]

★2 I _____ to go fishing with _____ dad.   [like my]

★3 You must _____ left and right when _____ cross the road.   [look you]

★4 My dad _____, 'Go and _____ in the park.'   [said play]

★5 We _____ to the beach _____ a holiday.   [for went]

★6 I _____ see the _____ dog.   [big can]

★7 Can you _____ the cat _____ the tree?   [up see]

★8 We _____ going to _____ wet in the rain.   [get are]

★9 She _____ sad and so were _____.   [they was]

★10 My dad said, '_____ and look at _____.'   [this come]

High frequency words – how many letters?

Read the words in the word bank. Find and circle them in the wordsearch. The words can only be read across, not up or down.

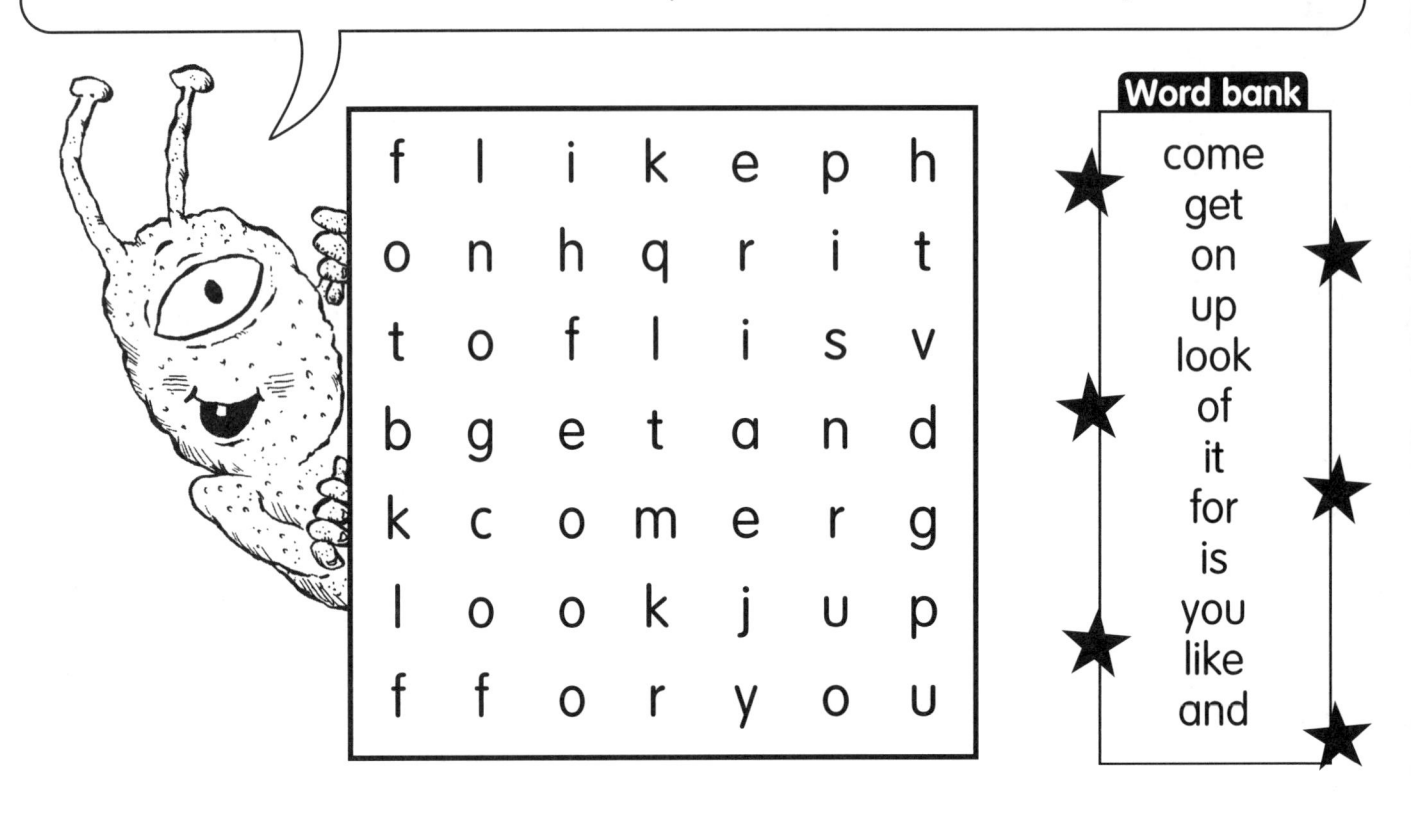

f	l	i	k	e	p	h
o	n	h	q	r	i	t
t	o	f	l	i	s	v
b	g	e	t	a	n	d
k	c	o	m	e	r	g
l	o	o	k	j	u	p
f	f	o	r	y	o	u

Word bank
come
get
on
up
look
of
it
for
is
you
like
and

Count the numbers of letters in each word in the word bank and sort them into the rockets below. One of each has been done for you.

2 letters
on

3 letters
for

4 letters
look

Phonics and Spelling 2

Sorting high frequency words by first phoneme

Blend the phonemes to read the words in the word bank. Find and circle them in the wordsearch. The words can only be read across and down.

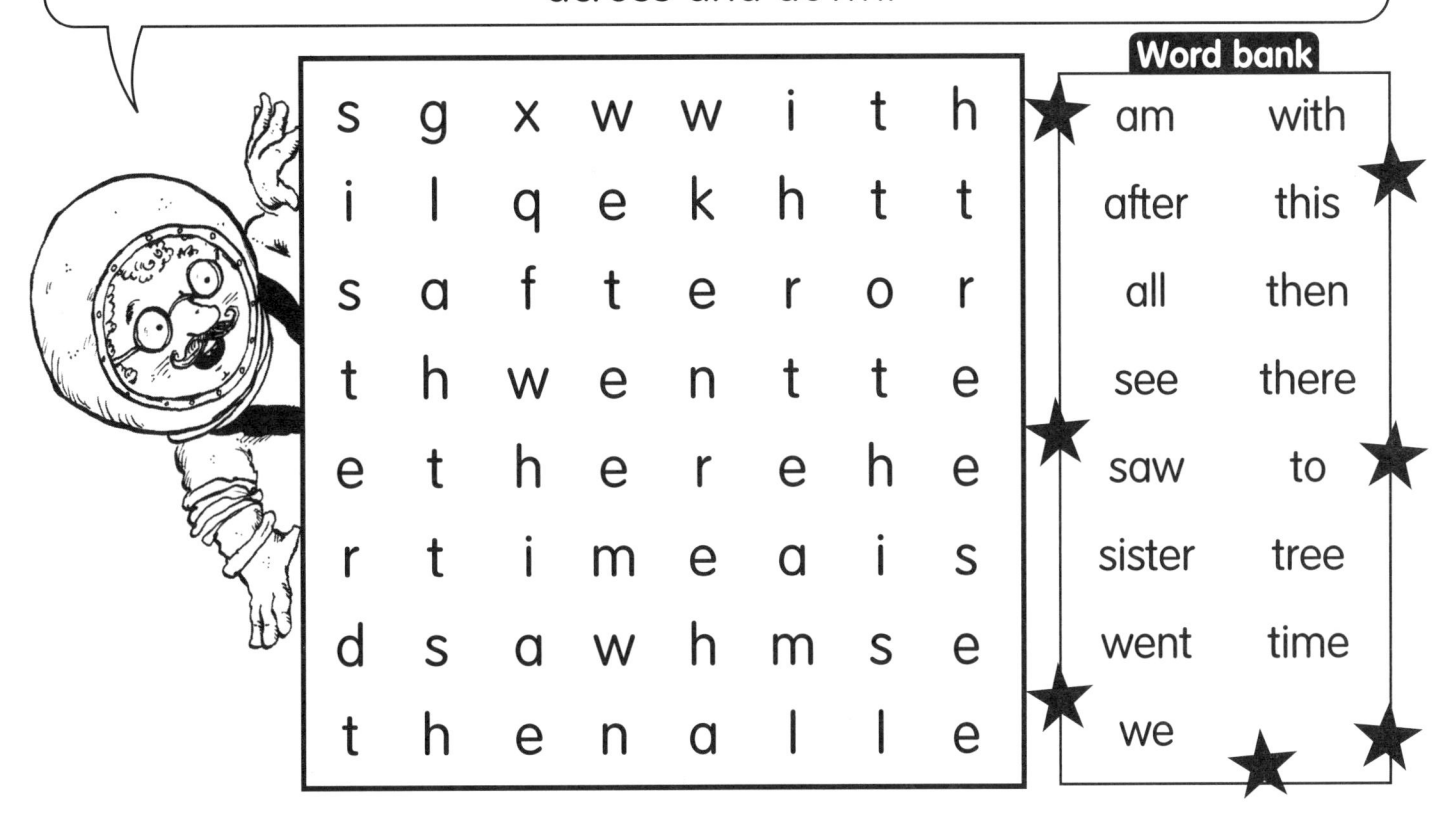

```
s g x w w i t h
i l q e k h t t
s a f t e r o r
t h w e n t t e
e t h e r e h e
r t i m e a i s
d s a w h m s e
t h e n a l l e
```

Word bank

am	with
after	this
all	then
see	there
saw	to
sister	tree
went	time
we	

Look at the first phoneme of each word in the word bank and write them in the correct boxes below. The first one has been done for you.

a | **s** | **t** | **th** | **w**

am | | | |

What can aliens do? (verbs)

We can do lots of things. What can aliens do? Blend the phonemes to read the words in the rockets. They are 'doing' words which are called **verbs**. Join each word to the alien who is doing what it says.

- hop
- dig
- jog
- jump
- tug
- cut
- mop
- run

How do aliens feel? (adjectives)

Blend the phonemes to read the words in the word bank. How do aliens feel? Look at the pictures and the words in the word bank. Write the words in the boxes beside the pictures. The first one has been done for you.

Word bank

hot   sad   sleepy   mad   happy   cold

hot

Upper and lower case letters

These are the upper case letters of the alphabet. They are also called capital letters.

A B C D E F G H I J K L M N O P Q R S T U V W X Y

These are the lower case letters of the alphabet

a b c d e f g h i j k l m n o p q r s t u v w x y

The letters below are in pairs. Write the missing upper or lower case letters in the stars to make pairs of letters.

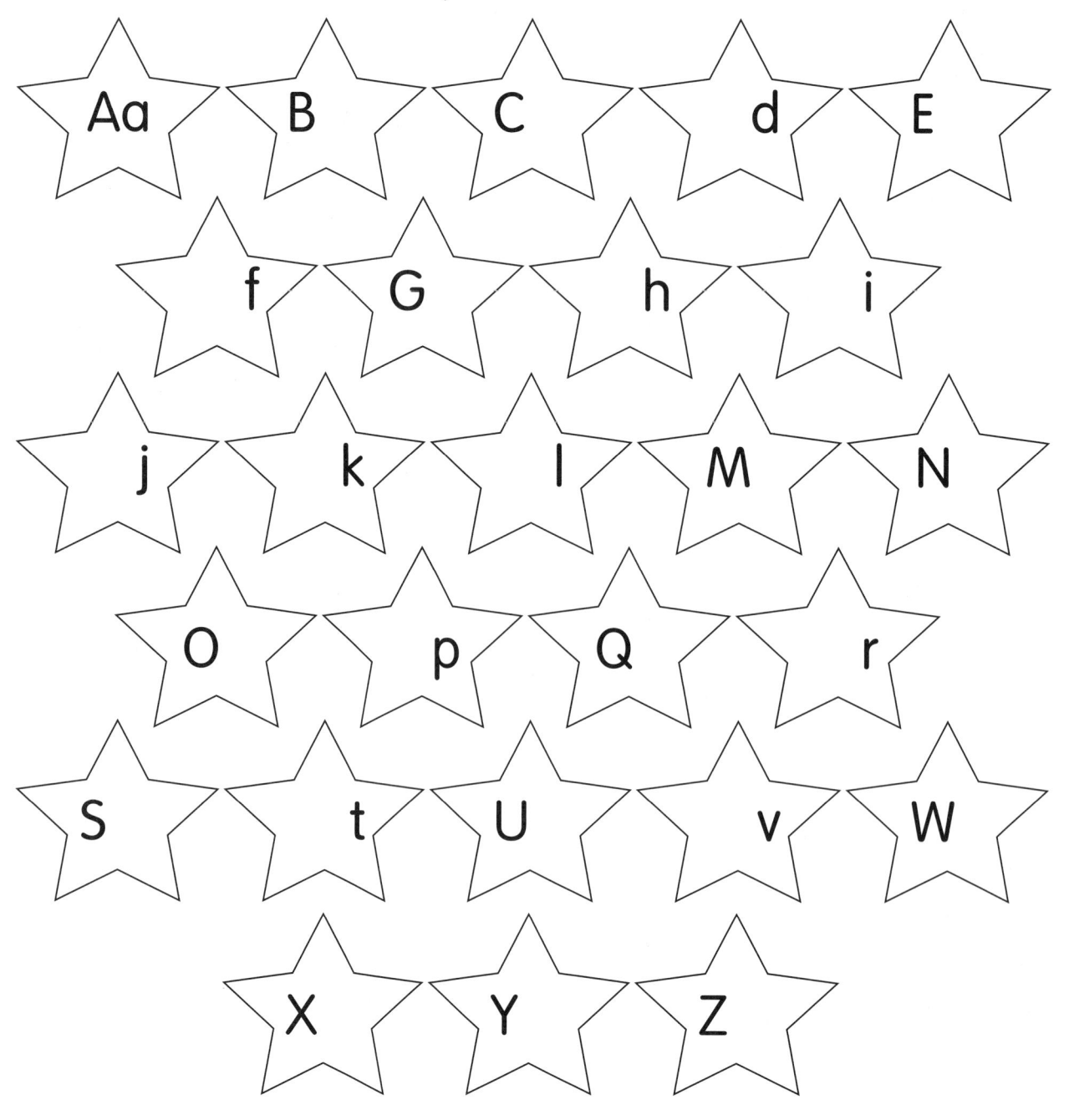

Aa   B   C   d   E

f   G   h   i

j   k   l   M   N

O   p   Q   r

S   t   U   v   W

X   Y   Z

Upper case letters

Capital letters are used for names of people, places, days of the week and months of the year. Circle the capital letters for the seven days of the week and write the missing phoneme for each day of the week next to it. Make sure that you use capital letters. Then do the same for the months of the year.

Months of the year

☐ anuary	January	☐ uly	July
☐ ebruary	February	☐ ugust	August
☐ arch	March	☐ eptember	September
☐ pril	April	☐ ctober	October
☐ ay	May	☐ ovember	November
☐ une	June	☐ ecember	December

★★★★★★★★★★★★★★★★★★★★★★★★

Days of the week

☐ onday   Monday

☐ uesday   Tuesday

☐ ednesday   Wednesday

☐ hursday   Thursday

☐ riday   Friday

☐ aturday   Saturday

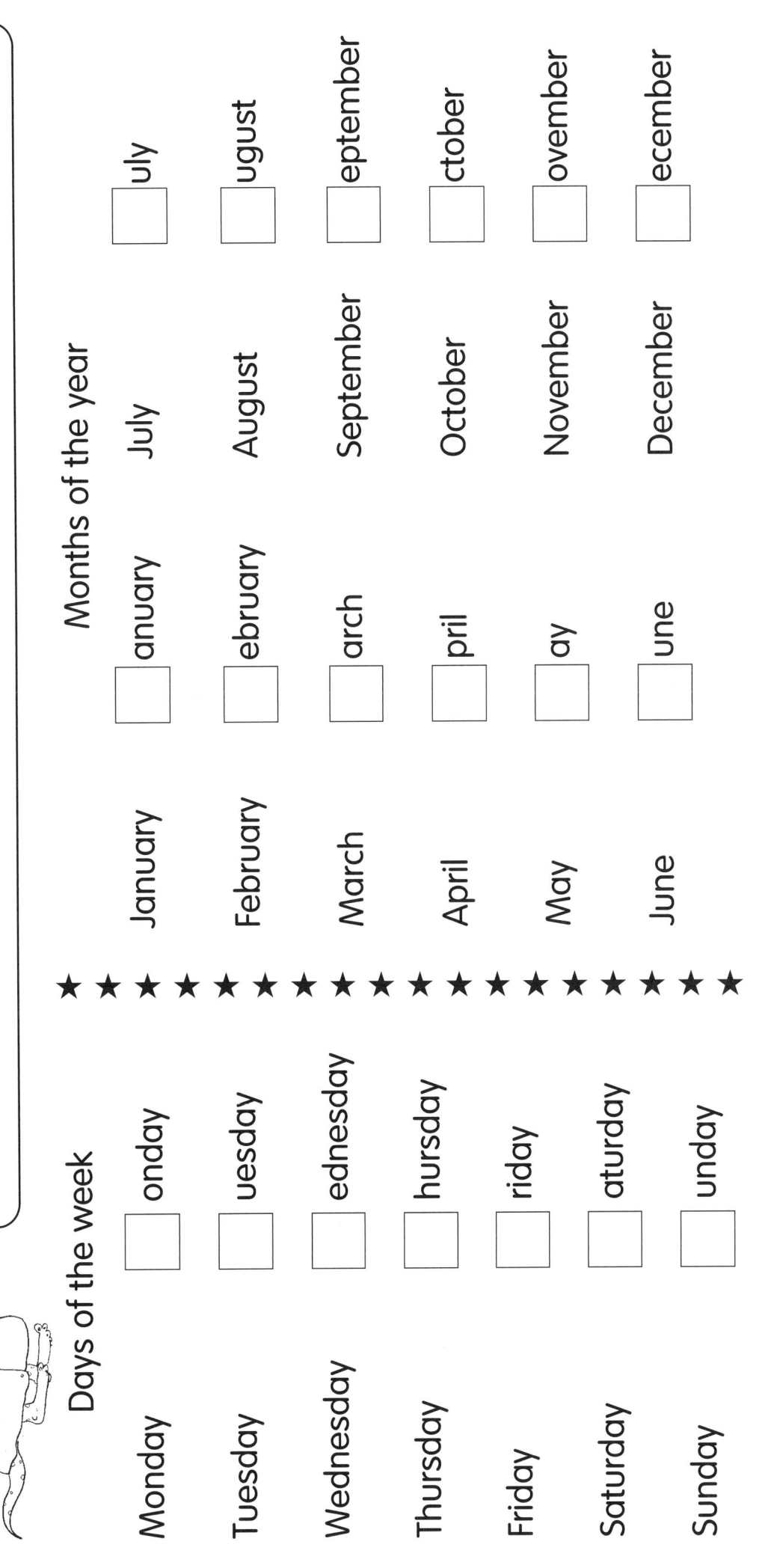

☐ unday   Sunday

Answers

■ **PAGE 5**

bed rub black
cat cut cub
dog bed drum
fox fat flag
go bug green

hen hat hop
jam jog jet
leg ball clap
mop jam plum
nut hen run

■ **PAGE 6**

peg cup pit
queen quick quack
rat rain tree
sun yes sail
tap pet trip

vet vest have
wet we went
box fix fox
yes yelp you
zip zoo zebra

■ **PAGE 7**

ant bag ran mat
red bed met net
in pig dig win
on pot hot stop
up bug drum lump

■ **PAGE 8**

a b c d e f g h i j k l m n o p q r s t u v w x y z

■ **PAGE 9**

a b c d e f g
h i j k l m n o
p q r s t
u v w x y z

a b c d e f g h i j k l m n o p q r s t u v w x y z

■ **PAGE 10**

def
ghi
jkl
mno

■ **PAGE 11**

pqr
stu
vwx
yz

■ **PAGE 12**

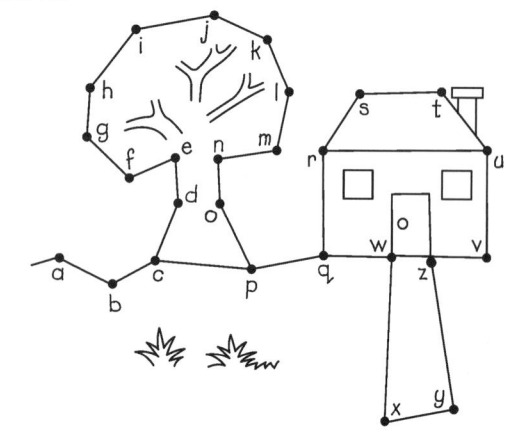

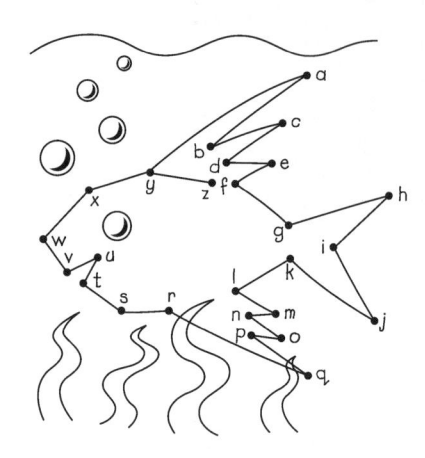

■ **PAGE 13**

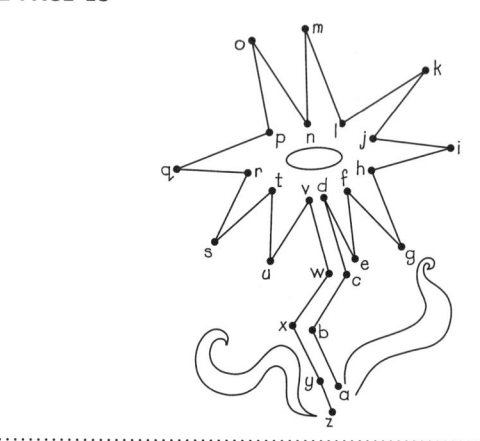

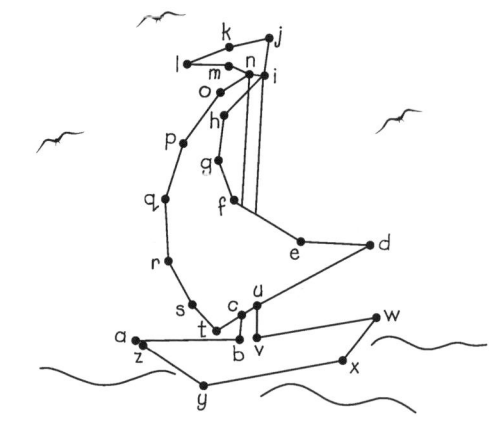

■ **PAGE 14**

bed   pin
cat   six
fox   ten
hen   umbrella
jug   web
leg   yacht
map   zip

■ **PAGE 15**

bat   net
cup   rat
fan   sun
hat   vest
mop   wig

■ PAGE 16

blow 
claw 
flag 
glue 
plug
slug

■ PAGE 17

crab 
drum 
grin 
pram 
train 
frog

■ PAGE 18

twins swan swing dwarf swim twelve

twins 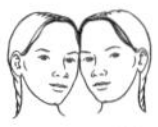
swan 
swing 
dwarf 
swim 
twelve

■ PAGE 19

1. The cut on my leg left a bad scar.
2. I like to skip to keep fit.
3. Some flowers smell nice.
4. A good card game is snap.
5. It is very rude to spit.
6. The bus stop is next to the shop.

scar
skip
smell

snap
spit
stop

■ PAGE 20

1. My cut began to **bleed**.
2. Mud is **brown**.
3. I like strawberries and **cream**.
4. He was a funny **clown**.
5. Catch the ball, don't **drop** it.
6. Birds can **fly**.
7. My painting had a red **frame**.
8. The fire began to **glow**.
9. My plant **grew** tall.
10. The princess was **pretty**.

■ PAGE 21

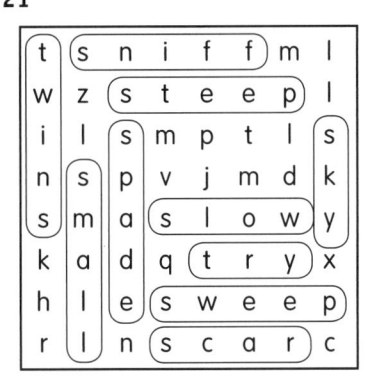

t	s	n	i	f	f	m	l
w	z	s	t	e	e	p	l
i	l	s	m	p	t	l	s
n	l	p	v	j	m	d	k
s	m	a	s	l	o	w	y
k	a	d	q	t	r	y	x
h	l	l	e	s	w	e	e	p
r	l	n	s	c	a	r	c

■ PAGE 22

1. I **chew** food with my teeth.
   My dog likes to **chase** cats.
2. I put the tins on the **shelf**.
   The **shop** sells ice creams.
3. I said **thank** you for the gifts.
   The old dog was very **thin**.
4. After my swim, I had a hot **shower**.
   The sun made a big **shadow** under the tree.
5. My **cheeks** were red with sunburn.
   Our teacher writes with **chalk**.

■ PAGE 23

screen
scratch
scream
scrub
splash
split

■ PAGE 24

spray   spring   square   squirt

■ PAGE 25

straw
street
string
strong
strawberry
stretch

■ PAGE 26

1. screw
2. splash
3. scrub
4. string
5. splint
6. spring

■ PAGE 27

three   3
throne 
thrush 
throw

■ PAGE 28

th	r	i	l	l
th	r	u	sh
th	r	ow
th	r	ee
sh	r	u	b
sh	r	ie	k
sh	r	u	g
sh	r	i	n	k

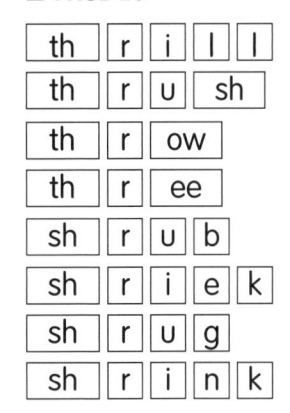

Phonics and Spelling 2

PAGE 29
1. I had a small **scrap** of paper to write my name on.
2. The **stray** dog had no home.
3. We had to **squash** the clothes into the small case.
4. The fish were in the **stream**.
5. I had to **thread** the needle to sew.
6. I **threw** the ball into the net.
7. He had a **splinter** of wood in his finger.
8. She jumps up and down as if she is on **springs**.
9. I **spread** the jam on my toast.
10. The mouse made my mum **scream**.

PAGE 30
wh ite	elep h ant	wh en
ch orus	wh ip	wh eel
wh ale	p h oto	telep h one

PAGE 31

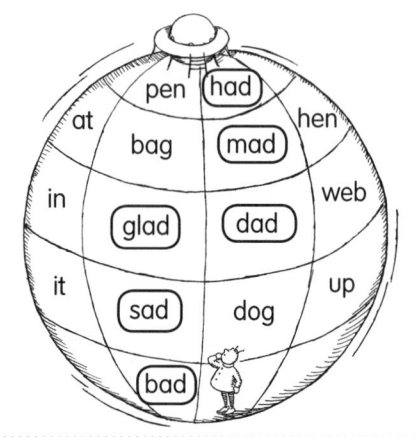

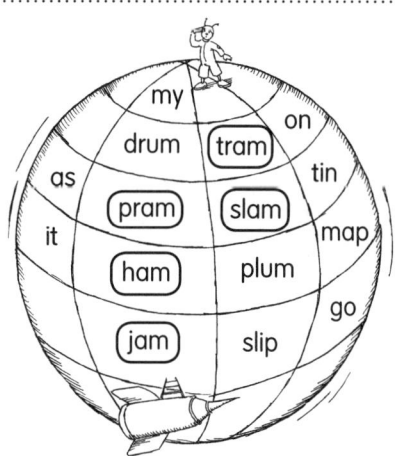

(Hot air balloon with circled words: had, mad, glad, dad, sad, bad; uncircled: pen, hen, bag, web, in, it, up, dog)

(Second balloon with circled words: tram, pram, slam, ham, jam; uncircled: my, on, drum, tin, as, it, map, plum, go, slip)

PAGE 32
can	clap	hat
plan	cap	cat
fan	trap	bat

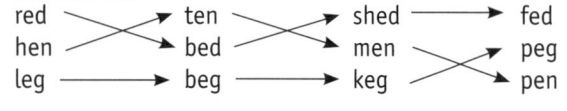

PAGE 33
red → bed
hen → ten
leg → beg
shed → men
bed → fed (crossing lines)
keg → peg
men → pen

PAGE 34
ip	in	it
pip	pin	pit
sip	bin	sit
nip	sin	bit
hip		hit
		nit

PAGE 35
dog	dot
log	cot
jog	pot
fog	hot

PAGE 36
shop	plug
top	bug
mop	jug
chop	mug

PAGE 37
drum	sun
plum	gun
gum	bun
mum	run
sum	fun

PAGE 38
1. bald
2. hand
3. card
4. gold
5. sand
6. bird

PAGE 39

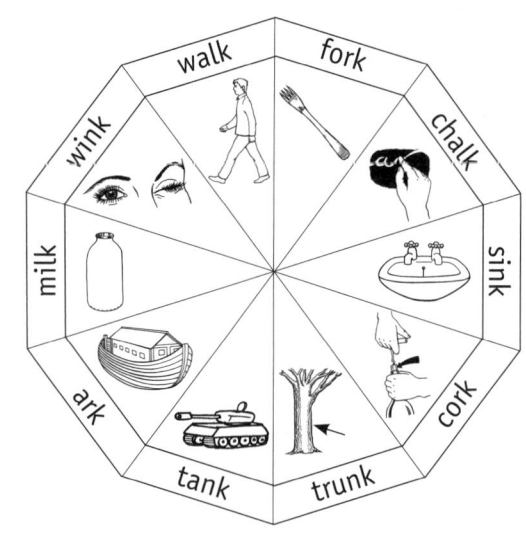

(Octagonal wheel with labels: walk, fork, chalk, sink, cork, trunk, tank, ark, milk, wink)

PAGE 40
1. There was no wind and the sea was **calm**.
2. On the island there were lots of **palm** trees.
3. Cows and sheep are **farm** animals.
4. The fire **alarm** went off when I burnt my toast.
5. The boat sank in the **storm**.
6. A movie is the same as a **film**.

PAGE 41
elp	ump	amp	isp	arp
help	stump	camp	wisp	sharp
yelp	thump	lamp	crisp	harp

PAGE 42
insect – act belt – melt
left – raft tent – ant
smart – cart fist – last

PAGE 43
church
torch 
match
bench 
witch
lunch

PAGE 44
king
sniff
peck
puff
ring
bell
dress
grass
lick
wall

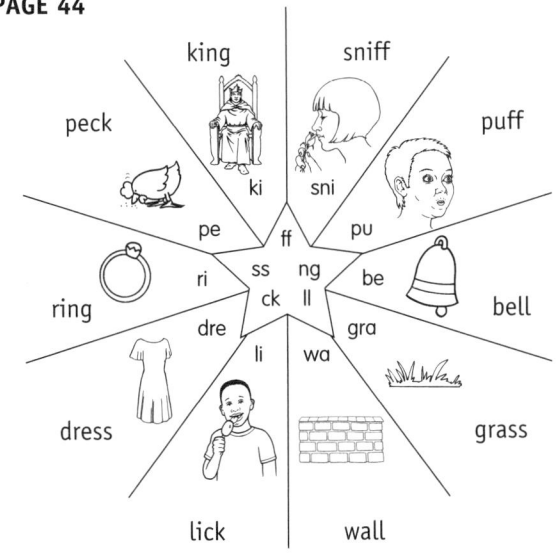

PAGE 45
sack	truck	wreck	sock	brick
black	suck	neck	rock	lick
pack	duck	check	block	pick
snack	luck	deck	shock	quick

PAGE 46
king – ring   rung – lung
fang – hang   ping pong – ding dong
wing – spring   swing – sling

PAGE 47
Hard g phoneme   **Soft g phoneme**
go   page
girl   gara**g**e
dog   cage
garage   germ
bag

PAGE 48
Monday, Friday, Saturday, today, clay, hay, away, pay, clay, way

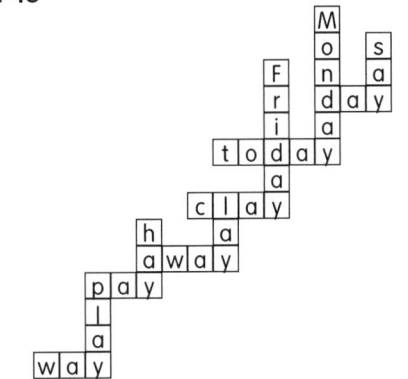

PAGE 49
safe   sail
rain   tray
pray   spade

PAGE 50
snail – tail   shake – make
chain – lane   tray – day

PAGE 51
green   she   me   sea   week   eat   bee

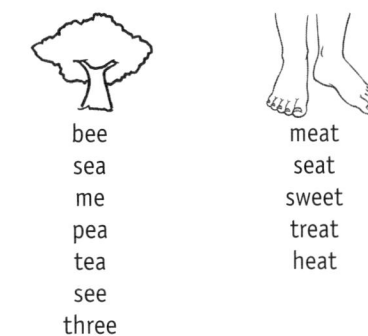

PAGE 52
bee   meat
sea   seat
me   sweet
pea   treat
tea   heat
see
three

PAGE 53
fry
smile 
tie
dive
night

PAGE 54
high
knight 
night
right 
light
fight

PAGE 55
dry – pie cry tie high
kite – night bite white fight
ride – wide side tide hide
mine – line fine nine shine

PAGE 56
boat
bone 
rope
go 
mow
soap 
toast
nose
tow

PAGE 57
boat	bone	blow	oak
goat	cone	bow	smoke
note	throne	toe	cloak

Phonics and Spelling 2

PAGE 58
screw 
glue 
moon 
shampoo

PAGE 59
blue – too
pool – rule
broom – room
spoon – moon
rude – food
boot – flute

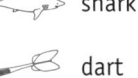

PAGE 60
shark  
card
dart 
barn 
farm

PAGE 61
claw 
jaw
paw
see-saw
straw
draw

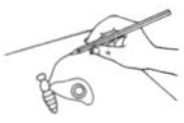

PAGE 62
bird
surf
fern
burn
skirt

PAGE 63
beads
meat
ice cream
leaf
beak
beach

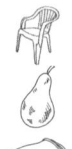

PAGE 64
chair
pear
pair
bear 
hare
where
scare
fair

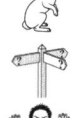

PAGE 65
town: frown, crown, bow.
slow: row, elbow, snow.

PAGE 66
pool: moon, tooth, boot, broom.
book: wood, hood.

PAGE 67
oy: toy, boy.
oi: coin, point, toilet, soil.

PAGE 68
door
sore
fork
short
horse
horn
storm
fort
before

PAGE 69
1. In my class there are lots of **desks**.
2. We need ten **sacks** for the sack race.
3. A bird flaps its **wings** to fly.
4. I have two **hands** and two feet.
5. Giraffes have long **necks**.
6. I like to throw and catch **balls**.
7. Our **tents** got wet in the rain.
8. Kings and **queens** have crowns.

PAGE 70
jumped
helped
locked
asked

1. I **jumped** up and down on my bed.
2. I **helped** my mum wash her car.
3. My dad **locked** the door with a key.
4. I **asked** my mum if I could go out to play.

PAGE 71
sinking
kicking
walking
jumping

PAGE 72
fairy
baby
dirty 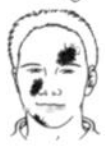
cherry
puppy
teddy

PAGE 73
1. hopping
2. button
3. toffee
4. kennel
5. robber
6. summer

PAGE 74
jumper = jump + er
duster = dust + er
quicker = quick + er
cracker = crack + er
older = old + er
taller = tall + er
walker = walk + er
recorder = record + er

PAGE 75
nicely
sadly/softly/sickly
quickly
neatly/nearly
badly
glumly
nearly/neatly
softly/sadly

PAGE 76
this = 1
mother = 2
door = 1
morning = 2
Saturday = 3
name = 1
suddenly = 3
window = 2
yellow = 2
garden = 2
light = 1
ball = 1

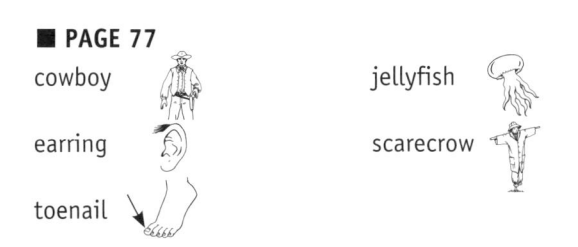

PAGE 77
cowboy
jellyfish
earring
scarecrow
toenail

PAGE 78
window, light, door, boy, girl, pen, ball, bat, chair, table, book, desk

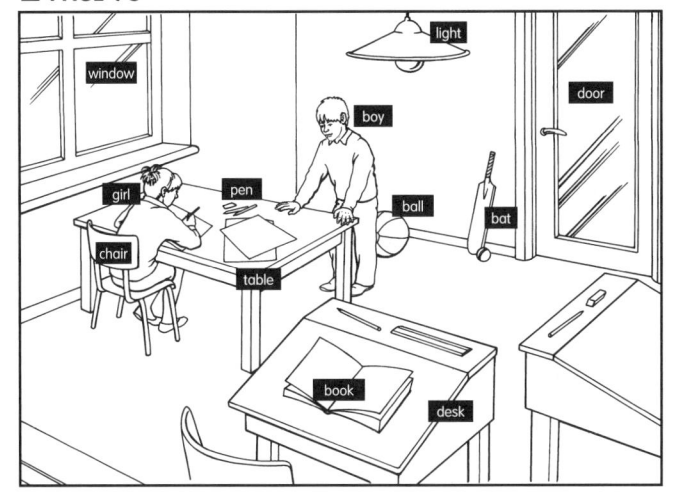

PAGE 79
roof, sun, cat, gate, bin, dog, tree, flower, path, grass, slug, peg, snail, pond

PAGE 80
short – tall   sad – happy
fast – slow   him – her
fat – thin   hard – soft
old – new   first – last
dry – wet   small – big

PAGE 81
undress
untie
unlock
unkind

discover
disagree
disappear

1. I **undress** when I have a bath.
2. To take off my shoes I **untie** the laces.
3. We **unlock** the door to get in.
4. The ugly sisters were **unkind** to Cinderella.
5. The aliens wanted to **discover** new planets.
6. My sister and I always **disagree**.

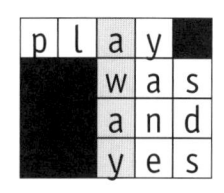

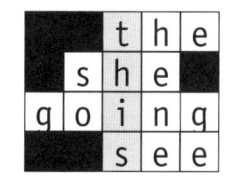

PAGE 82
(crossword: all, on, you, like / play, was, and, yes / the, she, going, see)

PAGE 83
1. My mum **and** I are **going** to the shops.
2. I **like** to go fishing with **my** dad.
3. You must **look** left and right when **you** cross the road.
4. My dad **said**, 'Go and **play** in the park.'
5. We **went** to the beach **for** a holiday.
6. I **can** see the **big** dog.
7. Can you **see** the cat **up** the tree?
8. We **are** going to **get** wet in the rain.
9. She **was** sad and so were **they**.
10. My dad said, '**Come** and look at **this**.'

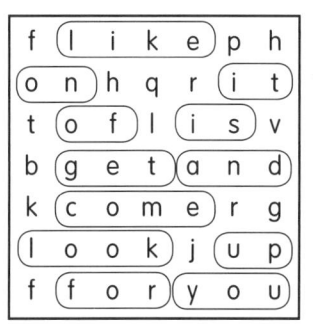

PAGE 84
(wordsearch)

2 letters	3 letters	4 letters
on	for	look
is	get	like
up	you	come
of	and	
it		

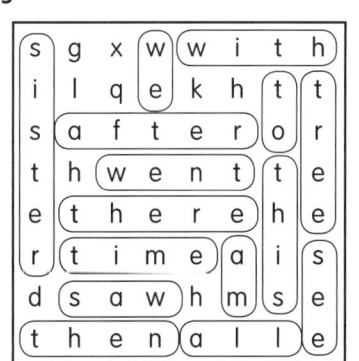

PAGE 85
(wordsearch)

a	s	t	th	w
am	see	to	this	went
all	saw	tree	then	we
after	sister	time	there	with

Phonics and Spelling 2

■ PAGE 86

hop –

dig –

jog –

jump –

tug –

cut –

run –

mop –

■ PAGE 87

– hot

– cold

– sad

– mad

– happy

– sleepy

■ PAGE 88
Aa
B**b**
C**c**
D**d**
E**e**
F**f**
G**g**
H**h**
I**i**
J**j**
K**k**
L**l**
M**m**
N**n**
O**o**
P**p**
Q**q**
R**r**
S**s**
T**t**
U**u**
V**v**
W**w**
X**x**

Yy
Zz

■ PAGE 89
Monday
Tuesday
Wednesday
Thursday
Friday
Saturday
Sunday

January
February
March
April
May
June
July
August
September
October
November
December